THE
BITCOIN
&
CRYPTOCURRENCY
WEALTH-BUILDING
OPPORTUNITY
GUIDE

Adam G. Koch

First Edition

Copyright © 2017 Adam G. Koch

Published by Adam G. Koch

All rights reserved.

ISBN: 1543060889
ISBN-13: 978-1543060881

DEDICATION

This book is hereby dedicated to my parents, especially my Dad who is lucky to have survived so many near death catastrophes in recent years, worst of all being 2016: Here's to you being around many more years, in hopefully better health. There's been a lot of good years, and a lot of bad years; but here's to making the best of the years that are left. You are proof that anyone can make it through anything if they are determined enough. And thank you Mom, for being supportive of me in all my ventures, especially through the many failures I've had all through my life before finding any measures of success.

CONTENTS

ACKNOWLEDGMENTS

I once believed Bitcoin would never be worth much. Then, I came to believe only Bitcoin could ever be worth much: Dozens of examples had proven me wrong, and I must fully acknowledge my friend known as "Bea" for helping me to see the light so that I may not continually pass up limitless opportunities in altcoins: The cryptocurrency opportunities of which are the very basis of this guide and why I've authored it.

I further owe a great debt of thanks to my best of friends, who are the best of muses, without whom there would have been no discussions or motivation for me to push onward towards success:

Tiffany Porter:
I couldn't have asked for a greater friend, nor a truer one; you helped me find my old self that I thought was lost forever; and you helped me back onto my life's path that I always was on but somehow had lost sight of; until you came out of nowhere and put me back on my proper path. I owe you a tremendous debt of thanks and gratitude for this not to mention you are the largest source of positivity and encouragement I've ever known.

Danielle Ahrens:
You have been a greatly inspirational muse and a great friend whose discussions have helped me see all the good that my work can accomplish.

Stephanie:
You've always been a massive source of positive energy for me, and great friendship; I didn't mean to drop off your radar for so long, so often, but at least you get to see what I've spent my time working on!

"Kunrad":
You've always been there to bounce ideas off of for nearly nine years, almost every day, too; so here's to the "gambler of all gamblers."

To all of my other friends: So many of you worthy of acknowledgement, but I can't write a whole book of acknowledgements! You are not necessarily less important or less appreciated. During this project, the people so acknowledged were instrumental in motivating me to actually finish this project that I never thought I'd see the end of writing.

"There should be no war upon property or the owners of property. Property is the fruit of labor; property is desirable; is a positive good in the world. That some should be rich shows that others may become rich, hence, is just encouragement to industry and enterprise."
-President Abraham Lincoln

"The real tragedy of the poor is the poverty of their aspirations."
-Adam Smith, Economist

"All the perplexities, confusion and distress in America arise, not from defects in their Constitution or Confederation, not from want of honor or virtue, so much as from the downright ignorance of the nature of coin, credit and circulation." – President John Adams

PART I : OPPORTUNITY & SKEPTICISM

This first chapter is intended to be a wakeup-call. A wakeup-call for what you ask? Opportunity. Much of our misery is due to missed opportunity, and most of our success is due to catching opportunity at the right place and at the right time, with the right attitude. What is the primary cause of missed opportunity? Skepticism which tells us opportunity could never be real for us, since it is something that *other* people always find, right? Particularly damaging to our cause is the fact that we cannot go back in time to fix our mistake of missing it since now is the furthest back in time that you will ever be. Every second which has passed, and is passing even now as you read these words, is a second closer you are to being too late for any number of opportunities. Hindsight is 20/20, but one man's hindsight is another man's foresight.

This chapter is also a motivational journey through opportunity; to explore what it is and means with the purpose being to illustrate the costs of ignoring or missing them as well as to demonstrate the vast benefits of seeking them out and leveraging them into success. If you don't see what it can actually do for you, there's no incentive to even bother with it; which there is a lot of incentive. I would bet money that cryptocurrencies have made more millionaires than all of the

MLM / Pyramid programs combined in their entire history, and with far less work and investment. It is human nature to be skeptical of new things, and to be resistant towards their assimilation into our daily lives, which is why we miss out on these things. Skepticism and doubt clouds our judgement and keeps us from seeing opportunity for what it is.

All people are equal in the eyes of opportunity; what makes real inequality is how our ambition, initiative, and mindsets as individuals are so different from one person to the next. If you give a hundred people the same gear, training, and opportunity; it is very likely you will have a hundred different degrees of successes and failures. There will be some who succeed spectacularly, and others who have failed spectacularly. Just as you cast sand into moving water and it stratifies by density and composition, the same is true about people when cast upon the waters of the everyday world.

Cryptocurrency is new to a lot of people, and it can be intimidating for the beginner as it can be difficult to grasp the concept at first. This is not surprising considering it really is a new breakthrough for the enabling of free enterprise and allowing for us to, in some regards, be our own bankers. We tend to hold a high degree of skepticism and contempt for those things we do not perceive as serious or worthy of our consideration and time. If you were to sit down with a piece of paper and write down everything you could have bought into but talked yourself out of buying that would have made you wealthy, I am sure it will be a lengthy list for the average person. When I write such a list, it actually is a disheartening and humbling thing to experience, but it causes me to focus on what I can do going forward so that I minimize the chance of missing out yet again.

Skepticism makes us not do things which we should do when it is the perfect time to do them, leaving us to do them when the boat has already sailed away leaving us to miss out on the bulk of the rewards; although there also are times when doubt insulates us from excessive and reckless risks.

The greater the risks are the greater the rewards will be; safety is not rewarded, because there is no risk in taking the safe route even though the safe route can be rather risky as well.

This is why the nine-to-five mentality usually results in mediocrity, and those who rise above mediocrity and the paycheck to paycheck syndrome have generally done something on the side to take some risks and dare to do something more than what is simply necessary to survive. There are people who adamantly believe we "exist only to work a career and to pay taxes" and who also justify living in mediocrity by repeating the "money doesn't buy happiness" bit...

No, money does not buy happiness, but I can guarantee you poverty doesn't either. Divorces, suicides, bad health, all too often are linked to A. debt, and B. missed opportunities that were so massive the people who missed them go stark raving mad as a result and cannot handle missing the boat. Everyone has their breaking points, and it is imperative that we as human beings find success before we reach those breaking points. Yet even though opportunity crosses our paths fairly often, we are oblivious to it. Even I am guilty of not taking opportunity for what it is, and it is painful to always miss out. Why must we have to work until our backs and health fail? Why must we put so much of our lives into not getting anywhere? Well, we don't have to. We just keep missing the signs which would point us to a better path, however you are now on the right track to stop doing that!

We don't grow up wanting to fail; we grow up wanting to succeed, but settling for a nine-to-five and not aspiring for more is not exactly success. A rising tide raises all ships... If you miss the boat and aren't on a ship, well, you are drowning in this thing we call life. Life isn't fair but we can do something about that, if we are aware of the fact there is something that can be done.

When we have it in our capacity to do the things we live for doing when we want to do them, that is true success. If you don't want to be rich, which there are those people, how much success is necessary for you to fulfill your destiny and to allow you to live the life you wanted to always have? That should be our priority while we are here on Earth, to be true to ourselves, and do everything we can while we can to build that success. That is what the American Dream really is, to be free of having to do that which we don't want to do so that we can be happy in the things we enjoy doing. Could you face your younger self if you had the opportunity to do so and honestly say you did not let "you" down? If you feel like you have let yourself down, now is the time to start changing that.

The goal is to no longer be forced to spend our lives doing jobs we hate because those things we love doing are not able to pay the bills. That's the difference between a job/career/business and a hobby. To be able to do everything you want should be what motivates you to rise above your lot in life and surpass this "mediocrity" which plagues society. Some say they love their jobs, and some actually do: If it weren't for the paycheck, would you still show up for work? Why work hard all your life for very little to show for it when you can stop missing every opportunity which comes along, and finally be on top of the world yourself for once? Millionaires are created every day of the year, why not you be one of them, too?

We live in a society that does not teach people about opportunity or how to leverage it; nor how to spot it for that matter. Some are born with this gift of seeing it and it is second nature to them; however, the majority of people just don't have this vision to see meaningful opportunity for what it is. It isn't an insult, and it isn't their fault as it is how society has engineered each new generation to think and look at the world. Once upon a time entire industries were built by people who had nothing but a few cents in their pocket and determination. Now, instead of the era of industry and empire builders, we've arrived at an era largely comprised of misery builders. Only we have the power within ourselves to succeed or fail, and we must assert our abilities to make it happen so we can break this cycle of proliferating misery.

"But the world can't function if no one has to work," is the argument that comes up next. It's not that big of an argument really. You see, there are people who if they could do anything in life for the love of doing it, would want to keep doing what they already do. For example, there are a large number of truck drivers who can't imagine living any other kind of life and the only way for them to ever give it up is when their health fails them. It is the freedom of the road, the grinding of the gears, and the whine of the diesel that gets into their blood and they don't want to live apart from it. As for ditch diggers, it takes capital to afford opportunities, and labor is the first price by which capital is bought; with capital being that which is necessary to go into business or otherwise invest in an opportunity, so let the young people work the jobs no one wants to work, worst case it would take them a few years to build up enough resources to expand into something a bit more lucrative and be free of it letting the cycle repeat again.

There are many failures before one finds success, so people go back to work until they can try again. Look at Nikola Tesla, he was taken advantage of by Thomas Edison so he resigned and ended up being a ditch digger, and then went on to be the most prolific inventor and I'd argue the most important one in history! Sure there will be vacuums in the economy if people no longer had to do their lousy jobs only for the income, but the world will always find ways to make do.

I owe my living to my ability to seek out opportunity. Yes, I've missed a lot of opportunity. Half a dozen times I could have been wealthy, but other people have always found ways to interfere and obstruct my participating in these opportunities. I've availed myself to enough smaller opportunities to survive on and in fact, I've made it an objective to write books focused around the intent of sharing the whole concept of opportunity and seeking it out. This is one such book. If you were never able to find opportunity, here in these pages you will find one of the biggest there is, and how to make use of it while you can!

The only thing I am selling, is this book itself and I didn't even ask a high price for it. What I make off of you ends there with royalties on the original purchase. In the long term, more people involved with cryptocurrencies will influence the market values to increase, but that is to all of our benefit if we are invested in them. I am not selling subscriptions, I am not pushing a service, what is within the covers of this guide is it. Your only obligation here is that if you buy the book, learn all you can from what I am presenting you. Even if you decide cryptocurrency is not for you, the seeds of seeking opportunity in all of its forms, have been sown.

There are many "opportunity guides" selling for a small fortune, but I am not that kind of author. In markets where a large quantity of new participants is undesirable, the information costs a fortune because those authors figure they will make their millions off of books and further figure that it makes up for losing a lucrative opportunity to the new people entering the market. I actually want to help people and I want to see everyone take advantage of this opportunity that is found in cryptocurrency. I am the kind of person that if I can do it, anyone can do it, because I have tried doing what other people do so successfully but I fail miserably, and I mean miserably at it all. If I find my own path, I succeed. Usually I succeed at things that are so simple, yet people assume it is more complicated than it actually is, like cryptocurrency.

For instance, the average person can go from one job to the next without any trouble. As for me, I spend years looking for work, and that doesn't pay the bills. So, I played video poker somewhat professionally for a few years and it paid more than I was making full time; it just required long hours and discipline to not make mistakes while playing. When the Video Poker was phased out due to regulation changes at the state level, I made it my goal to write a book on the subject, which after writing and publishing *"Gold Prospecting & Placer*

Deposits: Finding Gold Made Simpler", I did manage to finally finish *"Video Poker Profits from the Ground Up."*

I then was introduced to the world of stamps and stamp collecting, being a coin collector I scoffed at the idea stamps could be valuable. The same way many of you might scoff at cryptocurrency. There was a brilliant opportunity waiting for me, ignored by most people, but I was so biased against it until I ran into the right person that helped me see the opportunity and value in stamps. That is the basis for *"Philatelic Philosophy: Stamp Collecting Wisdom and Opportunity"* which I wrote and published; stamps are one of the few areas in the marketplace where you can literally build a massively valuable collection at low, zero, or even negative cost, meaning you can profit to build your portfolio of assets.

So you can see the pattern here. I have never turned a profit working a nine-to-five. I could not even get my online degree without Corinthian Colleges (Everest Online) ripping me off in a giant scam. Millions of people seem to get by on a nine-to-five. Millions of people seem to get their online degrees. Everything normal people normally do, fails miserably for me. So I must find non-conventional opportunities that require my non-conventional skills. I am not the only one who is in this situation, but the difference between myself and these other people is that I am willing to share what I know, not just what I think will sell and fatten my bank account, but what you need to know to actually put to use what I am bringing your attention to. Any trade secrets which I have, are to be entered within these pages. You will have my blueprints to be able to recreate my success in cryptocurrency by the end of this book.

In life, success means taking the path of least resistance. Some doors open, other doors are closed and only opened at great detriment to you if you insist on opening them. You have to embrace what works for you, and if you are fortunate, you will have a varied choice of many paths. The mindset to succeed is one of "If I cannot do these things, then what things can I actually achieve?" Why spend so much effort worrying about making things work which aren't working, when you can devote that energy into things which you can actually gain ground on?

Normally I would say all opportunities are not a good fit for everyone, but I must disagree in this instance. Cryptocurrencies are already being used as money, and they are traded the same way as stocks in the stock market. Actually they are a form of stock. People are putting Bitcoin into their IRA's even! Crypto's are shares in an idea, or a concept, in particular this means the niches the developers of the coins are targeting. It very much has become money.

There are risks, yes; however, they can be as great or as small as you wish to make them. Cryptocurrency affords you complete control over your strategy and how to approach the building of your assets. You can take the completely free approach, or you can squirrel away a percentage of your income into investing in them. Ten percent of your income each month for the last three years would have made you a fortune if you even just put it into Bitcoin! You can even build a massive mining operation for yourself if you want to become serious about it.

It is skepticism that will keep many of you from jumping into this life-changing opportunity in all of its various forms. We are worried about risk taking. If you do not want to be stuck in the rut that you are in, I am not asking you to replace your career or anything you are doing with any opportunity. If you want to break free from your rut, consider that everything you do on the side will make it easier for you to break free when the time is right. Build your airplane before you fly!

I didn't start playing video poker thinking I would in a million years replace my full time job with it. I was insulating houses and spending my days off at the casino playing video poker for relaxation. After taking a few days off due to fiberglass and my eyelids becoming infected from it, I decided my eyes were worth more to me than any job. The fact I was putting in ten to twelve hour days five days a week sometimes six, just to make less in two weeks at work than I made on the weekends at the casino made me consider the safety in quitting my job and pursuing the video poker.

Modern society has grown too comfortable and familiar with things that it on the average, views as secure which in reality are the opposite of what security is to the point an average nine-to-fiver is paranoid of taking any risks at all. Consider that if you aren't willing to risk pursuing any opportunities on the side, you are still taking risks. You are risking layoffs and downturns with no contingency plan to fall back on. Self-sufficiency is true safety and security, but you cannot be truly self-sufficient unless you find way to break free of the paycheck to paycheck mentality and lifestyle.

A career really becomes a trap, since work wears you down and tires you out to the point you have no time or energy to even look at other options, and opportunities right under your nose are often impossible to notice or avail yourself to because legitimately there are other priorities; family, obligations, any number of things. I am guilty of it too, and no I am not slamming hard work and those who have great careers, but why work harder for someone else when you can work smarter for yourself? Think of what reaching financial freedom would do for you and your family.

Imagine how much better the world would be should everyone be able to do what they want to do for a job instead of what they have to do for a job because they need the paycheck! You can see the difference all over the private sector, even to some degree in the public sector. Those who love their job do what they are supposed to do with greater efficiency than someone who despises their work. Also, how many people do you know who had a great career, bought a house, started a family, only to be laid off half way into raising their kids and paying for their house and cars? Many, many people. Chances are those are the same people who at one time told other people that they needed to find themselves a "career", too. What happens to you if your current career goes away? What would you do if you had no paycheck coming?

Consider your career as a vehicle. You can run it until it breaks down on you leaving you stranded; or you can work on a second vehicle in your spare time so that at least you can rely on it in addition to anything else you have figured out if the worst happens. For one thing, whatever wealth you can build on the side is in addition to that which you are already generating. What would this mean to you? Is it worth your spending a few minutes a day on something that can potentially make you financially independent sooner than you otherwise might or might not ever be able to achieve?

Since we have, if we are lucky, a hundred-year lease on life then why settle for mediocrity and condemn ourselves to living lives we would rather spend doing something other than what we are doing already? That is why this book is here, to turn that light at the end of the tunnel which we are content never to know is there, into a laser beam so it is able to reach you even if you don't reach it! Everyone can be doing something extra to better their lives and reach their dreams. To believe there is only work and survival, is to have a defeatist mindset. There is opportunity everywhere, for everyone; that is everyone who will see past their bubble of imagined security.

The reason so many people work hard all their lives and die broke goes back to a failure in society and how it collectively thinks. In order to correct this failure, a shift in the paradigm of thinking and teaching is necessary. I am writing this book because I want to see all of you become successful, and this is one opportunity that by helping everyone be successful in it we help ourselves be more successful in it. The difference between the successful and unsuccessful people is that those who are successful are not wasting their time and money complaining about how unfair life is, instead they do something to make it more equitable to themselves. It generally takes time, and it often takes money to make success; but you must also find the opportunity. If you have neither time, nor money, you are still in luck because this opportunity will require as little or as much as you wish to put into it to not totally miss out on; and it is all explained in this book.

There are countless "opportunities" which you hear about regularly. Many are designed to benefit the people who thought them up, or the people who are successful at pitching the opportunity and recruiting others to participate. As a result, the word "opportunity" can often draw a bad reputation and evoke negative thoughts. When I mention opportunity, you probably immediately think of things like Amway, Prepaid Legal, etc. Yes, they have made lots of people successful. However, success doesn't appear to be typical or easily attainable for the average person who will stumble into them. Sure they have great products, but good luck building a business with them. My experience in such opportunities is that you need to know a lot of people and have a lot of family whom you might go to and try to sell things to.

The beauty of the cryptocurrency opportunity is that there are no programs to sign up for, no monthly membership fees just to be a part of it; there is literally no mandatory overhead or expenses just to be involved unlike the aforementioned programs. There is nothing to buy nothing to sell. Cryptocurrency exchanges and marketplaces often have referral programs but you make only a small commission on the typically small fees that are charged by the platform. However, it is easy to build a referral base since people signing up are wanting to use the service anyways and registrations are always free. Exchanges and marketplaces operating on cryptocurrency only exact their fees when transactions occur, which is very fair. You are not paying for something you didn't use or are deriving no benefit from.

A major factor involved with people being able to build success in MLM's is there being a mandatory subscription or fee structure which subsidizes those in your up-line. Even if you fail at selling product, it is possible to succeed by selling others on joining these "opportunities." These types of programs generally charge a monthly fee or require you to subscribe to the service in order to be eligible to sell the products. Often, it is a burden of hundreds of dollars up-front. I feel much better about bringing to your attention, an opportunity in which there are no compulsory costs.

I've met people who were so successful at MLM programs that they were able to quit their jobs after a couple of years and pocket half a million dollars a year as a result of their success. Not everyone is cut-out for that kind of opportunity and those kinds of results are not at all typical, especially for people like me. Doable, but not typical. It is a tremendous investment of time and money just to see if you have a chance at succeeding in such programs. There is no need to invest time and resources into cryptocurrency to wonder if it will work. There is no if. There is only get involved in whatever capacity you are able while the getting is good.

I've personally given a full attempt at making sales opportunities work; I am not a sales person and network marketing is not my thing. Once upon a time I was excellent at selling, but those times in my life have passed. I would rather operate in a passive business model whereby I do not have quotas, and where I can actually help a lot of people. Writing books has turned out to be my niche, and it fits my needs for a passive business model and amazing opportunity; but now also, has cryptocurrency. It has proven to be of such a revolutionary opportunity that not even I have failed at it, and mediocrity has tended to be my middle name throughout life. Yet, here's something that has allowed me to position myself for outstanding success.

Whatever I could do, everyone else was always doing better. It is particularly annoying when I have figured out how to do one thing so well and all of a sudden it quits working for me even though I have not done anything differently. One of the great lessons in life is that it is possible to do everything correctly, everything you are supposed to do, and still end in failure. The universe tends towards disorder, and we are sucked right along with it whichever direction it is wanting to take us. There is but one solution to this problem; sticking with it, finding what works, and seeking every opportunity we can find along the way.

Opportunity, and making use of it, is the key to defeating our "status quo". It's been said that we all come into the world with nothing and with nothing we go out of it which makes us all equal in that regard. The only reason our lives vary so much from person to person is due to the degree of which people have seized opportunity or ignored it. Opportunity is the lever with which we might move our world, and it is the intent of this publication to show you the places to stand from which you may apply your greatest leverage with the most force to make the largest positive impact in your life that this, or any, opportunity can possibly provide you.

You will probably have doubts well throughout reading this book. It is healthy to view things with skepticism, and our lot in life can be of such a nature that we can't imagine breaking free of it. I've been there and in fact, I still struggle with it. It is very demotivating when you can have so many years of such bad luck, and to be walked on and stabbed in the back by so many people, especially relatives. I've been railroaded out of so much by so many people; but in the end, my failures are all chalked up to missed opportunity. Not doing what I should have, when I should have, because I didn't know any better or how to make it happen with limited resources. I've been so demotivated, that this book is nearing a year in the making. When I started out, Bitcoin was a mere $700. Now, I am rewriting and revising my chapters as necessary to make them more valuable to my readers; Bitcoin was $3,000 when most of the following chapters were written originally but now it is a whopping $7,500. *Now doing the proof-edit before publishing just a week or so later, Bitcoin is now $10,000+.*

I want to stress that Bitcoin is a huge opportunity yet, but it is very volatile. If you buy a large quantity at $7,500, and it drops to $5,000 or $3,500 you will feel sick; but the trend always is that it never goes lower than previous lows, and it is getting harder to mine by the day, and there is so much demand for them and so little supply. There are people publicly going on the record stating that Bitcoin will reach $1 million dollars by 2020 (Bill Gates said this according to numerous articles I've ran into. I can't verify it obviously.) A PayPal executive recently said there is a greater than 50/50 chance Bitcoin is already worth a million dollars, and that was in a reputable news article!

Eventually yes, Bitcoin is a million-dollar coin. If we were to go into a coma and wake up in ten or twenty years and check the price of Bitcoin, we will be in total shock. In ten or twenty years from the publication of this book, never mind a hundred or more years passing, it is astronomical to think what might come of the Bitcoin value. So, if buying Bitcoin, I will tell you straight up to figure out what percentage of your income you want to put into it, and do not fail to follow through. It will go up, it will go down, but it will average out and in the end you will win. $10,000 BTC is around the corner, then it will go for $25,000... Once it hits $25,000, it won't take long for the hype to drive it to $100,000.

The stable price of Bitcoin for a year or so had been around $1,000 a coin. I couldn't justify spending $1,000 for a Bitcoin. Then, it dropped to $700, and I won a Bitcoin in a casino off a 0.01 BTC wager. My laptop died, and I had no way to afford a replacement. So guess what, I had to sell my Bitcoin and add a few bucks to it yet, and buy my new laptop. No computer means I am unemployed; my livelihood is my computer.

It quickly headed to $3,000/BTC after I had sold. So in many ways I feel like I've missed the boat, but I haven't missed it. Bitcoin is only one facet of this beautiful opportunity, as you will see in the coming chapters. It is very disheartening however, that this laptop went from being a $1,200 machine, to being about a $10,000 machine thanks to that money not being able to stay in BTC where I needed it to remain. This of course is the very definition of an opportunity cost, by the way. If I kept the BTC it would have cost me being able to work; and selling it for the laptop means it cost the BTC to be able to keep working.

In 2010, I don't know that anyone took bitcoin seriously. There were some people who knew it was heading for hundreds of dollars but I don't think any of them then were able to foresee it heading for the thousands and tens of thousands of dollars a coin. I am going to attempt to write this book with the perspective of what it would have taken to convince me in 2010, when Bitcoin was new, to have gotten involved and not to have missed out to the degree I did.

We may possibly have missed Bitcoin to a great degree but not completely; however, there are new coins skyrocketing every day! There are literally dozens of cryptocurrencies I had looked at and thought, "I don't think it will do anything", and that is dozens of times I could have turned a few dollars into a few million, rather literally. Take your pick; $0.05 Litecoin going up almost to $100.00 a coin. Monero, Ethereum, all doing similarly. There will always be more such opportunities, but unless we retrain our minds how to think and approach these things, we will continue to miss them. It is all too easy to dismiss something with a low value as being worthless, and it gets a person every time.

My great uncle told me the story of how once he owned around four-thousand acres of water frontage on the river, and gave it away because all he wanted was the timber, which he logged, and didn't want to have to pay taxes on the land afterwards. The value he once seen in it was already exploited and no longer existed, and was content to tell everyone the land was worthless, so as he told me, he gave it away for the taxes. Turns out, that same land became worth hundreds of dollars a square foot when people started wanting to retire or build vacation homes to be able to live on the water. It is human nature to not see the value in things which are valuable until long after it's too late. Traditional thinking had blinded him to any future possibilities. Hindsight is 20/20, but lucky for us cryptocurrency is an ongoing opportunity for the foreseeable future. Think of how old traditional money and banking is, but there are still opportunities here and there, right? Imagine how young cryptocurrencies are now, and how exponentially greater the potential opportunities are with them where the future is concerned!

The biggest critics and skeptics are going to say that the American Dream is dead, or rags to riches is impossible. It just can't happen, right? Wrong. Maybe it is difficult, and very hard to obtain, but it is possible and it does happen. The hardest part is convincing yourself to participate in any given opportunity while it is still good timing. The perceived risks can seem so much greater than the actual risks; we can only spend time once. We live in the moment, heading to the future, but the past is sealed so we try to do what we think is right and what we think we need to, especially when we are wrong. It is possible to be burned by so many opportunities and so many people, that we just don't want to try anymore. This, however, is different from most opportunities.

As for rags-to-riches; I personally know a couple that I am good friends with whom had turned their last $100 into what became a multi-million-dollar empire of retail stores. They didn't whine how unfair life is, nor did they cling to their last few dollars. They didn't say the world owes them a living. They never went on any government handouts, either. They dared to pursue a vision in the most traditional American way imaginable.

It did take them years of working for nothing all day to build what they did; the song Taking Care of Business is not an exaggeration at all, but a literal truth of what greatest success stories have gone through, and what the average nine-to-fiver does not understand or even acknowledge.

Workers feel like the rich are getting rich by stepping on them to climb their way up. No, the rich got rich by sacrifice and risk taking; it is why to some degree owners resent their employees, for their employees tend to feel entitled and exploited but have no clue as to what hardships the owners themselves endured to build a nice big company that can offer a relatively safe career to its workers that do not appreciate the effort to be able to build something that can offer a job.

If it weren't for entrepreneurs and capitalists, there would be no jobs. Government does not create jobs, (except in its own agencies which are far overreaching in size and scope) the private sector does. So long as people can't find their own way in life, jobs will be necessary because people have to eat, afford housing, and raise their families. When a poor person wants a loan to start a business, they go where? To a banker, or a rich person who can finance the venture without sacrificing their own ability to survive in the process.

Rich people do not stuff their money in their mattresses, rather they stuff it into the economy, building new buildings and factories and developing new markets for new products and services. This is what creates the jobs most of the world so desperately needs in order to survive, not to mention they are driving innovation. Who among you can gather a few people and empty your wallets into one pile and say, "Let's start building smartphones and compete against Apple and Motorola!" It just doesn't work that way. If you truly had the abilities to make a phone, you would have to seek out the capital, a lot of capital just to get going, and it would be years before you were able to keep anything for yourself. If you destroy the wealth of the few who were successful, you destroy the ability for them to feel like they can afford to take risks on people who want to borrow money to do big things with their great visions, particularly in things that banks are prohibited for lending money for.

The job you don't like but have to have because your survival requires it, only exists because someone originally sacrificed most of their time they could have spent with their family or doing whatever else they valued, and put everything they owned on the line. Everyone who works for themselves that has achieved anything great literally has done their time of "working for nothing all day" for much of their business owning career; five to ten years is a common duration to pass before business owners have something left after paying overhead to no longer have to work all day for nothing and be rewarded for their labors and lost time.

There are hundreds of thousands of people in this country who "make" millions, but after the tax man takes his cut and after paying operating expenses, they are very lucky to even be a part of the middle class heaven forbid they can actually keep anything they have earned for themselves. One does not simply become a part of the mythical one percent without having to work hard and sacrifice a long time to achieve it.

There are rich people who are totally lazy and had their fortune fall into their lap, and yes, they have earned our contempt. It is better to not be upset with what others have and you don't, but labor to build yourself up, instead. The thing about wealth though, is if you didn't build it yourself, you haven't a clue how to make it grow further and it is why lottery winners are in the poor house a year or two later. I am actually going to teach you how to build your wealth through cryptocurrency, and by building it yourself, you will appreciate it, and be able to keep repeating it as necessary until you are comfortable with your success and able to achieve everything you want to achieve.

Devoting even a small amount of your spare time to finding and participating in any opportunity can very much make the difference between vacationing on your couch due to it being the only place you can afford to visit, and sitting on a beach somewhere watching the sunsets and feeling like a winner because you finally made it. You have to dream big, and these dreams will not happen unless you take some steps towards making them happen. Fortunately, you do not have to create a whole new industry like Vanderbilt and Carnegie did, nor do you have to make a new invention like Edison; you merely have to open your mind to this phenomenal opportunity which is before you now, in this book.

A truly great opportunity can be participated in equally by everyone regardless of who you are or where you come from. (The exception of course might well be China, with their great firewall keeping everything out they don't want in, including cryptocurrencies and websites pertinent to them. Even in Vietnam, Bitcoin itself is banned entirely, yet the people still buy and sell it on the streets and in shops in secret. If communism can't completely stop cryptocurrency, there is very little that can.)

Bitcoin has allowed people to bypass all manners of regulations, and that is the kind of trait which is valuable in any currency. The free market principles are always at work as surely as the universe has laws it operates under and will always find ways to reign in overregulation. Cryptocurrency is one such mechanism for enabling free market ideals to keep working. No matter how totalitarian a country is, there always will be a black market. Black markets are not evil, they are just the free market continuing on despite the whims of a nation's leaders, although most of the stuff that should never be for sale is available through black markets so therefore they garner a bad reputation and end up scaring people away from them, along with the types of people that are involved.

I myself failed in the beginning to make a proper assessment of Bitcoin and associated currencies that came afterwards. It was a fifty-fifty chance of me deciding correctly (either I would do it or I wouldn't do it) and I chose wrongly. In betting against Bitcoin, I came to learn that I had bet against human nature and the fact it always seeks a new way to finance its vices and circumvent the rules we find in society, which is necessary in preserving liberty by the way. I do believe in laissez-faire, do as you want to do but let me do as I want to do, though there are a few small exceptions: As long as everyone's activities do not interfere adversely with the lives of anyone else, there should be no regulations or laws restricting us in our ventures and enterprises. We need fewer regulations and fewer laws. Let people be free enough to succeed. Now, kids can't even set up lemonade stands, they have to have inspections and permits first!

(Yes, black-markets notoriously have used cryptocurrency, but there will always be black markets. Don't let that dissuade you, for at one time in history just about everything has been illegal somewhere. Books were burned in Nazi Germany; alcohol was illegal during prohibition in the USA. Would you believe there are places in the United States where adult toys are illegal? As sad as that is, there probably is a poor soul in prison somewhere because they were pulled over by the police with a carload of vibrators. Draconian laws are numerous, and growing in number by the day. It is my hope people will wake up and choose liberty over tyranny. Just because something is illegal does not make it wrong. The real wrong is usurping the natural rights of individuals on the supposition they may abuse them.)

The more against "the system" something is, the greater chance that it will potentially succeed and be seen as tremendously valuable. Bitcoin was just one of those great innovations which ran entirely against the system and indeed has proven itself. Gold and silver run against the system too, which legally they were supposed to always be our system if you read the constitution, but thanks to Woodrow Wilson along with the Federal Reserve and Internal Revenue Act of 1913 which he signed into law, that all changed forever which is a discussion for another book which I plan to write telling the story of why sound money is necessary for a society to prosper. This act paved the way for the total destruction of sound money which was the ever watchful guardian of private wealth and prosperity.

There will always be attempts from those in power to curtail the liberties and safeguards which things like gold and silver provide against a progressive government agenda.

President Franklin Delano Roosevelt seized all privately owned gold under his first executive order (#6102) upon entering office in 1933, though $20.67 in non-redeemable paper money was paid for each ounce of gold seized. In 1934, gold was revalued to $35.00 an ounce, meaning in a year's time the people who lost their gold to the government were robbed of around 40% of their wealth almost overnight. It wasn't until the 1970's when gold was deregulated and again legal for Americans to own. When something serves the interests of the people too well, government will always try to stop it.

Bitcoin cannot be seized or confiscated in the traditional sense, and it is unclear if even the Great Firewall of China can stop cryptocurrency completely. Then I've heard rumors about China wanting to ban all cryptocurrencies and create their own state operated cryptocurrency which all of their people are to use!

People love their freedom even if they do not fully understand the concept of freedom at times; Bitcoin is essentially a financial freedom movement at its very core and just like an idea, it will always waft across the highest walls and the most secure borders. I did not even think about these things in the beginning. I did not know these were things to even consider. I seriously underestimated Bitcoin's ability to preserve and enhance liberty and my skepticism would not allow me to see the real value inherent in something completely intangible.

Had I dared to even put a hundred-dollars into Bitcoin in the beginning of the coin's life, I would be wealthy beyond my wildest dreams. All that would have been required to convince me to do so would have been to cause me to recognize Bitcoin for the vehicle it was; a vehicle enabling mankind to sneak through the regulatory firewalls which are ever obstructing opportunity and prosperity. This is the real root of freedom; being able to use our wealth how we want to. We earned it, we suffered for it, no man and certainly no government has any right to tell us what we may use our money for, yet they do because they have us entirely reliant upon money they create out of thin air, that they regulate.

We have almost come full circle: It's how the tea ended up in Boston Harbor. Britain and King George the Third were essentially looting the colonies by placing Americans under such heavy financial and regulatory burdens beyond which could be tolerated, and eventually people did something about it. Chief among the tyranny was the refusal to allow a fair money system to operate in the Colonies. Something will always be done when it gets to that point regarding anything, so here we have arrived at throwing traditional banking into the digital harbor.

It isn't a new concept to do what we want with the money we've earned and the capital we have built for ourselves; rather it is an old one that once was championed as "free enterprise". Corporatism has infiltrated and replaced real capitalism and free enterprise. It is why we have so much red-tape preventing anyone from undertaking any venture without a mountain of permits and licenses. Big business has learned how to protect itself from competition by making sure no one can come in and compete, and if they do it will be so costly they won't possibly survive trying; all while the regulators are bought and paid for to serve *them*.

Laissez-faire doctrine is the only doctrine truly enabling us to achieve our greatest potential. It is what enabled industrious people to go from rags to riches. America used to be the nation of free enterprise, and we are slowly returning to it after decades of government overreach and red tape; but our problems of today are largely due to this country turning its back on what made it great in the first place: Sound money and economic freedom. Both of which are enabled by cryptocurrency because cryptocurrency, while to some degree is being regulated, is reasonably impossible to enforce regulations against.

Government can freeze bank accounts and seize assets.

However, money is controlled either by banks or by governments or both. Cryptocurrency is decentralized, there is no one place they can go and shut you down at. They would literally have to seize all of your hardware, all of your internet accounts, and even then they still couldn't possibly find all of the places you may be hiding your cryptocurrency. All they can do is enforce regulations concerning the conversion of fiat money into cryptocurrency, or vice versa. Money is necessary in any form we can find it in, and even more valuable is to be able to use it as we see fit. Government does not know what is best for us, we do.

Money is said to be the root of all evil. This is not true at all. It is the love of money that is the root of all evil. Money itself is a tool bearing the traits of its wielder, neither good nor evil in and of itself. The world runs on money, society cannot function without it. Bartering is declared by many people to be superior to the way things are done now, yet it is so flawed; whilst a cow is worth upwards of a thousand dollars today, would you work a twelve-hour day in the hot sun to only be paid in a few pounds of beef? I should think not. You could trade the beef maybe, but would you be able to find a taker before it spoils? You also can't squirrel away fruit and nuts for your retirement, either.

Whilst people continue to prosper their governments try to become more devious in how they use money as a way of controlling and influencing the people living under them. An honest commodity money is ideal; people say it isn't because the rich just hoard the money. Yet, fiat is believed to be acceptable and inflation is mistaken for prosperity; "Oh, everyone has more money now than twenty years ago!" I am sorry but someone is failing to consider the loss of purchasing power due to the inflation. Gasoline was also $1.25 a gallon twenty years ago (in the 1990's), and minimum wage was around $5.00 an hour. Now, we've seen gasoline up to $4.00 and almost $5.00 in recent years but it has settled in around $2.75 per gallon currently. The minimum wage has not risen to $10.00 an hour even though gasoline is more than double.

Consider further that gasoline was at one time $0.25 a gallon. It would have been a 90% silver quarter containing what right now is $3.00 worth of silver at about $17.00 per ounce for silver. This means gasoline is actually slightly cheaper in terms of real purchasing power. So, it's not that prices have gone up, it is that fiat money is confiscating our wealth and making us poorer every year that we use it.

If your wage-increases and investment returns do not keep pace with inflation, you are losing money and getting poorer. A $100 bill will not buy as much in five or ten years as it will buy now. In terms of real wealth (sound money), prices aren't changing much at all. An ounce of gold in ancient Rome would buy you a nice toga, sandals, even a sun dial, and a day out on the town. Now with the same ounce of gold you can still buy a nice suit, shoes, wristwatch, and still have enough for a night out on the town. Commodity money was scrapped for doing exactly what it is supposed to do; preventing confiscation through inflation, and making people wealthier over time and not poorer.

(Our founding fathers understood this, and it is why in section 19 of the Coinage Act of 1792, Congress had made it a felony punishable by death to debase our coinage, or in other words to make our money to contain less precious metal than prescribed by law. An honest money is necessary for a free and prosperous society to thrive. In fact, it worked so well we did not have a federal income tax at all in the 1800's. 1913 was the first time we were stuck with the income tax, and it was only to prop up the Federal Reserve which in turn enslaved our nation to the bankers.)

If a commodity money is hoarded, deflation sets in, which makes the circulating money more valuable, meaning what little you do have will buy more making you wealthier. This isn't really a bad thing. It is only terrible if you insist on circulating more paper than you can back up, which is precisely what happened with the advent of the Federal

Reserve. If wages go up on sound money systems, it is because everyone actually is wealthier and the economy is doing better.

Bitcoin is deflationary in nature and it is touted as a selling point! We will all be richer over time just by having it! But gold and silver are bad because they are deflationary? All fiat money systems have ended in failure. Ancient Rome had debased its coinage so badly towards the end, there was very little silver or gold in their coins. Then you have the hyperinflation in Germany, all brought about by the Weimar Republic attempting to print their way out of debt because they had so many obligations after losing WWI. Never mind the fact our dollar has lost 99% of its purchasing power since 1913. Let's face it, whoever owns the most paper money, loses. This is true everywhere you look in the history books.

Deflationary money is traditionally seen as a problem despite the fact that in the United States anyone back in the day was able to round up their own gold and silver in whatever form they found it or owned it, and send it in the United States Treasury to be minted into coins with a small portion retained by the treasury with the majority returned to the person to whom the metal belonged, in the form of newly minted government money. I once had the worst looking silver ore assayed and it ran forty troy ounces per ton of ore as is! Imagine, stuff I would have thrown on my driveway, containing that much silver to basically a pickup load. That is huge! Gold and silver standards put the origination of money into the hands of We the People, not bankers who have a racket to run like the Federal Reserve is doing. Cryptocurrency is attempting to do digitally what mankind used to do physically in the real world; allow us to be our own bankers, and to again participate in the creation of currency.

Actual current (fiat) money is not purely digital and it is highly regulated since the government that issues it seemingly has the power to control how its people are able to use it; so cryptocurrency is naturally a good choice for things like gambling, and transferring large sums of money under the radar for instance. Some cryptocurrencies are impervious to all attempts to track the transactions and who spent or received them!

I expect these truly anonymous cryptocurrencies to eventually surpass Bitcoin in value someday, simply because it is better to have total anonymity than only some, combined with other issues that plague bitcoin as well. The whole point of cash, digital or physical, is that we can do what we want to do, especially if it is purely legal and honest, without having big brother write down and build a dossier on everything we do and buy in life. There seems to be an assumption that every day people will not have a large quantity of money unless they are doing something illegal, which is a most flawed way of looking at things. Right and wrong cannot be measured by the metric of legal or illegal, because actual right and wrong is not arbitrary like legal and illegal is. Too many things which are not crimes, are turned into crimes by a greedy judicial system and an oppressive legislating body who seek to insulate the "in" crowd from ambitious outsiders.

Cryptocurrency in general can be considered a pseudo-commodity money in that of each of the cryptocurrencies which exist have certain parameters governing how they are initially created (mined) as well as how many will exist before new coins are no longer mineable. There are any number of other factors which can be considered to impart value to the currency, or in some instances there are traits which actually negatively impact the value and usability of the currency. Generally, you will not find two cryptocurrencies exactly the same, by the way. There are copycats and clones of successful currencies, but they vary somehow in their implementation.

What gives it an "almost commodity" status is the fact every bit of the cryptocurrency is accounted for in a system with a self-auditing mechanism, and it cannot be counterfeited. Exploits have in the past been used to double-spend the same coinage effectively giving the exploiter free stuff, but the coins themselves that weren't actually spent are a pure loss to the recipient, and the coin supply is not permanently increased; think of it as digital shop-lifting. A double-spend would be like writing a check for something, but copying the check and depositing it back to your account before the merchant can deposit and clear the funds. It is a form of theft, but numerous precautions exist to prevent it from happening.

There are bugs found from time to time with certain altcoins which are detrimental, but usually these are repairable. Gold and silver cannot be counterfeited, either. In other words, cryptocurrency is as close as you are getting to having a purely digital equivalent of gold and silver. This being said, there have been attempts at backing cryptocurrency with gold, but the main attempt I am aware of is known as Eldorado (ELD), but has since been defunct since the defect was found in Cryptonote algorithm based currencies.

The alleged bug in the software allowed counterfeiting of coinage, however I could not recreate or independently verify this was actually possible. Someone may have concrete evidence, or actually did succeed at doing it, but for the here and now I can say it just as easily could have been a "hit job" on Cryptonote. Coins utilizing this algorithm were either patched, or abandoned. (ELD) ended up being completely abandoned. Bikercoin (BIC) ended up being abandoned but a new coin on an entirely different platform was created, with the ticker (BIKER) though who knows if it will do anything. Monero (XMR) and Bitcoal (COAL) upgraded their wallets and software to block the alleged bug, which ultimately is the honest way to do it.

It is at great costs of time and even of money or capital that some of us acquire various currencies so it is always a sad thing when one becomes worthless; but diversification can be your friend. Just for the record, one ELD was equivalent to one (supposedly) redeemable ounce of Gold. I do not know if anyone actually successfully redeemed theirs though, the project died in its infancy, but supposedly it was a reputable company and they had a repository in Canada.

Cryptocurrencies are not the first digital money that ever existed. Liberty Dollar, operated by The National Organization for the Repeal of the Federal Reserve Act, and e-Gold.com both operated successful digital currencies backed entirely by solid gold and silver, even platinum; that is until Bush Forty-Three signed the Patriot Act into law. It became (one of) the tools used to destroy and seize the assets of Liberty Dollar and e-Gold. They operated slightly differently, though.

Liberty Dollar may have been left alone, save for the 2008 Presidential Election, for which they endorsed Ron Paul for president, and put Ron Paul on copper, and silver rounds as part of their endorsement. There were massive quantities ordered by customers; it was a very popular item. However, just after they arrived but before many could ship out, the FBI raided the headquarters in Indiana and at the same time they raided Sunshine Minting, in Coeur D'Alene, Idaho to seize all of the bullion and rounds owned by NORFED. Liberty Dollar had letters from the various government agencies from earlier years saying NORFED was not doing anything wrong, that they were not counterfeiting, or doing anything illegal. Liberty Dollar was the very example of what financial currencies should be and it did at no point violate the Uniform Commercial Code. Yet, the initial allegations were counterfeiting despite the government already stating they were not counterfeiting. The metal has been, and is being, returned to the rightful owners at present time; which are those who hold warehouse receipts and redeem them.

Digital Liberty Dollars were redeemable for the metal that backed them; the paper Liberty dollars were physical warehouse receipts, which conveyed title to the bearer of the indicated quantity of gold or silver which was held in reserve until that note was redeemed. I remember the day of the raid very well, though the details are foggy after so many years; I was about a day away from launching a paid to read email website that was going to run primarily on digital Liberty Dollars. The raid happened, and well, there went that idea. There were lots of paid to do this or paid to do that websites, but none of them were running on digital Liberty Dollars. I think they were actually called Electronic Liberty Dollars, or ELD's, but either way same thing. You see, that is the story of my life; a vast opportunity before me, and a monkey wrench is thrown into it out of nowhere. It almost never fails.

e-Gold actually was physical metal circulated digitally. It has very low service and transaction fees making it uniquely suited to micro-transactions. Paypal charges a minimum of around fifty-cents to receive a transaction. e-Gold was a fraction of a cent to send or receive. The cause of e-Gold being raided and shut down? Anti-money laundering laws and the Patriot Act. They basically had to prove none of the transactions or users were aiding or abetting terrorists or enemies of the United States, and the government essentially wanted the use of Gold and Silver in this instance to be regulated the same way banks regulate the Federal Reserve dollars, which is ridiculous. For one thing, I will arguably state that more PayPal transactions are made every day that aid and abet terrorists than in the entire combined history of e-Gold and Liberty Dollar. Cost of compliance goes up, logistics become unmanageable, all because of regulations. Regulations choke innovation and stifle prosperity.

It is all a war on sound money and private property. How dare anyone privately own metal, and use it in transactions via a mutually agreeable contract to denominate sales and purchases in units of precious metal! The private sector is ready, willing, and able to give us sound money that will work as it is intended to; and that is what spells its downfall. Sound money works for we the people, unlike the Federal Reserve Dollars, which are ever benefitting a progressive government and elite "banksters". Our founding fathers understood this principle of central banking and paper money, but the elite were so cunning and powerful that our American money system was conquered by them. George Washington issued the following warning:

"If ever again our nation stumbles upon unfunded paper, it shall surely be like death to our body politic. This country will crash."

It is this principle as to why we have in the Constitution of the United States the following:

*"**No State shall** enter into any treaty, alliance, or confederation; grant letters of marquee and reprisal; coin money; emit letters of credit; **make any thing but gold and silver coin a tender in payment of debts**; pass any bill of attainder, ex post facto law, or law impairing the obligation of contracts, or grant any title of nobility." (Article I, Section 10)*

Nothing but Gold and Silver were ever to be used as money, and never was paper money to be issued:

"Madison, agreeing with the journal of the convention, records that the grant of power to emit bills of credit was refused by a majority of more than four to one. The evidence is perfect; no power to emit paper money was granted to the legislature of the United States." –George Bancroft

Further exposing some of the fraud which our fiat money system actually is; from our own congressional record:

"Some people think the Federal Reserve Banks are United States government institutions, they are not government institutions, they are private credit monopolies."

–Congressional Record, May 11, 1972

And one last quote everyone should be aware of from the chief architect of our current fiat money system:

"By a continuing process of inflation, governments can confiscate, secretly and unobserved, an important part of the wealth of their citizens." –John Maynard Keynes

Imagine that... We went from "taxation without representation" to "taxation with inflation".

Without gold and silver able to be used as money like it

should be, cryptocurrency is functioning in lieu of sound money and filling this void to a large degree making it the biggest dog in the fight for the cause of liberty and sound money, even though intangible resources cannot be considered sound by the very definition of intangible. The only benefit imparted by cryptocurrency to the sound money movement, is the fact it is a very real revolution aimed at reducing our dependence upon our fiat moneys of the world. Anything physical can and is regulated to death. There are movements to restore us to a sound money system that at least could run parallel with our fiat system, but ideally we would be able to replace it entirely.

Cryptocurrency is also a sort of digital fiat money in that some developers went in together and "decreed" the coin to exist by creating the code and algorithms that established the cryptocurrency, but while fiat is inflationary cryptocurrency on the long term is highly deflationary. All of these coins which end up being utilized and survive to see their usage grow, have scarcity and versatility working in their favor. It amazes me that something decentralized is centrally planned, but like a herd of wild animals being let loose, good luck finding them all again!

Despite the fanatics, cryptocurrency will never replace actual money or even gold and silver for that matter. A true money is a stand-alone platform; it will always be what it is, readily identifiable, easy to use, and requiring no other technology or aid to use it than the form it is in. It is of necessity something that can be utilized anytime, anywhere, anyplace, regardless of whether you have access to the internet and electricity. Tangibility is key to money being good as a money; if you can't hold it or touch it, you don't actually own it. "I own Bitcoin, though!" So, can you point to the specific ones and zeros of binary code on your hard drive and say, "These, these are my Bitcoins?"

When Blackbeard's pirate treasure is dug up someday, all of that Gold and Silver is going to be in roughly the same condition it was in when he buried it; which means you could spend it and use it as if it was put there yesterday. If on the other hand, you bury a hard drive or a flash drive with your Bitcoin on it, or even a paper wallet or a "physical" Bitcoin which has Bitcoin "loaded" on it like a prepaid gift card or debit card, it is a stretch to say that these are timeless, and you can't transfer or otherwise confirm and utilize Bitcoin transactions without the grid functioning. The mechanism for turning those "physical wallets" into digital ones again may simply not exist in a dozen years or whenever you may someday need to convert them into a useful form. Physical gold and silver are always at the ready, and virtually indestructible.

Sure, some people are out there who will say "stocks are safer, they are real!" But are they real? The reality is, do you get anything back if the company which you own shares in were to fail? I've held many a failed company's stock and the answer is no, unless you happen to own a preferred stock when it goes under; in theory at least. Supposedly the liquidated asset proceeds are distributed towards paying off preferred shareholders in the event of a corporation going out of business. Standard share-holders get burned. Is paper wealth any more tangible than bits of data on a computer drive? It isn't.

Strictly speaking in terms of tangibility, there is no difference of intrinsic value in stocks when compared to cryptocurrency. Stocks may represent something real but you can't buy one share of Microsoft and show up at their headquarters and say "I want to take home my 'share' of your company." Stocks almost become paradoxical with regards to this fact in that they imply ownership of something you cannot actually take possession of (unless you buy 51% of all shares). It all ends up being worth what someone else will pay, and usually it is arbitrary, based on reactionary logic.

Cryptocurrency is actually superior to stocks since there is effectively no way for them to be excessively regulated like the stock market is. In order to be able to day trade last I checked, the stock brokerages required minimum of $25,000 cash value in your portfolio due to Regulation T as they call it. It may have changed since then, however that puts day trading out of reach of people who could greatly benefit from it. You can day, and night trade cryptocurrency all you want with any amount of investment. The crypto markets run 24/7/365; a feature I absolutely love about them. Yes, weekends are sacred for various reasons; but finances literally in this day and age can be a matter of survival especially outside of business hours. A five-day week of banker's hours is insufficient to properly serve society's needs in our current era, so again we have free enterprise solving a market failure!

Bitcoin is a difficult concept to wrap one's mind around at first if you are not exposed to it very much before getting involved, and to understand the "altcoins" and the associated opportunities, need to know about Bitcoin which means that it will be explained. It is virtually impossible to go into complete depth on Bitcoin, but I will at least provide the basics necessary for the scope of this book and for you to reach your objectives.

If you think of any crypto coin as a share of stock, it much simplifies the learning curve since most people are familiar with the stock market. Whichever stock brokerage you use, yes the cryptocurrency exchanges work the same way, except you will not be able to short sell without finding someone who will lend you the coins you wish to sell short. If only I had known a few years ago to think about altcoins in terms of penny stocks, as I will also explain in greater depth with the next parts of this book, it would have made so much more sense to me and I would have rushed to the computer to make sure I got in on it while I could!

Everyone new to this crypto-world tends to be confused and tripped up by cryptocurrency because it sounds high-tech and confusing with the language, or the fact it seems completely foreign to us and requires so much technology. It really is as simple as thinking of the cryptocurrency tickers as stock tickers, and thinking of the marketplaces for these currencies as stock exchanges of sorts; except you are not buying into a company, but rather the ideas and niche markets the currencies were made for based on how they appeal to people and what use they serve to those that have them. It is the vision of the creators of the coin that set the stage for success or failure.

Alas, the whole phenomenon seems ridiculous to a rational mind until it is thoroughly studied, reviewed, and then the spaghetti of threads starts weaving into one grand tapestry. The "big picture" will come into focus, you just need the right lens to look at it through, which is the purpose of this book's existence; to be that lens.

At present, Bitcoin is worth nearly seven ounces of gold. When I learned of Bitcoin, it was worth maybe a tenth of an ounce of silver. There are over sixteen-million Bitcoins mined currently which exist. It was inconceivable that Bitcoin could result in the creation of hundreds of millions of ounces of gold worth of wealth out of thin air. You could have told me this would happen seven years ago and I would not have believed it. Just as you probably won't believe it when I said Bitcoin will go to $10,000 and then work its way up into the millions of dollars per coin. How can something purely digital and unbacked, unredeemable be worth an ounce of gold, let alone nearly seven ounces of gold? (*Bitcoin just did pass $10,000.00 a coin as I proof edit this part of the book.*)

I should have known that having such a large portion of the population so content and desensitized to use their plastic to pay for everything, many of whom perhaps never having handled paper money in years, would be perfectly content with a money that cannot be seen or felt at all, ever! I already knew we are heading for a cashless society which I much despite the idea, and that's been the elite's plan all along to solidify their stranglehold on the world. Once (government /

central bank) money is purely digital it can be controlled in total, and our ability to buy and sell can be destroyed to any degree the status quo wishes. It was also my fault that I forgot P.T. Barnum's wise words; "A sucker is born every minute."

Sure it seems foolish now to doubt such things, but it is a small consolation to people like me who missed out, that there are countless people I run into every day who had laughed at their opportunities which had at one time been within grasp for them! These people could have once bought Starbucks (or as I call it, Starburnt) stock for next to nothing only to have it explode into a cash-cow of returns. As if that's not bad enough, I've met a lot of people who are dragging themselves along in low gear burned out from working hard, and they tell me they should have bought Microsoft stock back in the beginning but thought at the time Microsoft wouldn't do anything meaningful so they ignored it.

Yes, computers at one time were considered such a novelty that people figured they might go away, just as I made the mistake of figuring Bitcoin would go away as the novelty it so certainly had to be. Actually, computers were sold to hobbyists for years without a practical purpose, leaving people to invent a practical use for them! The pattern will be found everywhere in this world that history repeats, and only the fools and suckers fall for the old line that "there is no sure thing." There are lots of sure things, we just aren't trained to spot them because we ignore the past usually. You literally have to learn how to think and perceive every day events all over again. It isn't easy shifting the paradigm into a pair-'a'-dollars! I couldn't help the pun!

Missing a life-changing opportunity is the difference between working until you die having achieved none of your dreams, and having an early enough retirement that you can actually enjoy your life and spend time with your family or those who matter to you. A lot of people are married to their careers and end up regretting not taking the time out to make a family, or cross a few things off the bucket list, but that is what the all mighty dollar does to people. There are shortcuts, but we are taught not to find them for the elite need their tributary slaves to keep laboring on into the day and night so they can be taxed and controlled through debt and monetary policy.

I've known people who were years ago offered a thousand bitcoins for a thousand-dollars, and are now regretting not taking the offer. I mean, why would a person turn down an opportunity to buy anything so cheap since chances are the average person has lost far more than that in one night at a casino, and you know a thousand bucks in a casino will have a snowball's chance in hell turn into a million bucks. Yes, I will try to hoard my money when I have it and not invest it as I should, and end up squandering it anyways. What you think you should do and what you should do are not the same thing all of the time, otherwise we would be rich already!

Sure we are creatures of instant gratification, if we can't have it now we often don't want it at all. That is why get rich quick schemes have made their creators wealthy, and perhaps even why savings are at an all-time low. Everyone wants to get rich quick, but no one wants to take a risk and hold onto it for a few years and see where it takes them. Some say they will not get rich by hanging onto their money because they have so little of it anyways, that they might as well spend it. The beauty of cryptocurrency is in it being a tremendous opportunity which has such a low cost to be involved with that there is nothing keeping all of you from building your portfolio of cryptocurrencies, except maybe a lack of knowledge and not knowing what exactly this opportunity is or what it can do for you. Safely building up a portfolio of coins that is not likely to fail takes some knowledge and understanding of the dynamics which make up the marketplace. It takes knowing opportunity cost, and what every single dollar can actually do for you if properly leveraged. This is the main purpose trying to be achieved here with this publication; to arm you with the knowledge sufficient to conquer this realm of opportunity, and break you free from the shackles which bind us to jobs that make us live in stress and poor health day in and day out.

I underestimated the inherent worth of cryptocurrency and largely ignored all associated opportunity in it, not just Bitcoin, but all altcoins: I ignored cryptocurrency in the same way those poor souls ignored Starbucks and Microsoft stock. I knew it would be useful in circumventing financial regulations, embargos and other such restrictions on trade and commerce; but I had believed I missed out as the price quickly rose into the hundreds of dollars, and I did not perceive the altcoins as ever being valuable. I felt the opportunity had passed beyond my reach. Little did I know, the opportunity was just beginning especially after all this time. Had I bought a single bitcoin at the $100 mark, when I was screaming after selling a bundle of them at $20.00 each; As of today, it was worth over $8,000 for one Bitcoin. Is it a bubble?

There are no signs it will crash, and so much money is in line waiting with buy orders at various prices; if the entire stockpile of existing BTC were dumped, it is unlikely the market would crash very far. Do not, however, be under the impression BTC is not manipulated. Cryptocurrencies are routinely manipulated by very skilled operators, their means and methods are genius, and just maybe, I will write another book someday detailing these mechanisms. Although I will tell you there are trading "bots", software that automatically buys and sells based on certain algorithms in order to, over long periods of time, impart gains to the operator of the software. The higher any currency goes, the more impossible it is to actually manipulate it successfully.

Gambling and black market activities have a ridiculously high amount of capital going through them, and these are the two primary uses of cryptocurrency, particularly Bitcoin in the casino market, so there could literally be no limit to how high it can go because of this. Add to it, cryptocurrency is going mainstream and merchants everywhere are adopting them! The mining opportunity for Bitcoin has passed into the unprofitable category. It takes a vast fortune in hardware to be able to mine any appreciable amount of it. $8,000.00 Bitcoin now... It is harder for an $8,000.00 something to double in price, than for a $0.008 something to double, triple, or more in value. *(Of course BTC is now over $10,000.)*

There are routinely altcoins which go from ten-thousand coins to the dollar to a dollar each and even ten-dollars a coin after a single year, sometimes a couple years. I have seen in the past eight months or so, several coins rise from 0.01 of a Bitcoin (BTC) to being worth 0.060 of a BTC. The strategy you will find in this book primarily is concerned with growing our investment through altcoins and trading them, though traditional methods will be covered for the Bitcoin purists.

If it simplifies the concept of many different currencies, it may be considered like this: Bitcoin is the first coin, and as such it has a home field advantage. Why go to competitors when you can go to the original? As such, it is regarded as the "Gold Standard" of cryptocurrency, and is the basic universal reserve currency upon which all other altcoins are ultimately valued. Litecoin (LTC), Monero (XMR), Ethereum (ETH), can all be considered as silver since they are lower value, and easier for people to acquire. Then, you have the copper's. In stock terms, these are the microcaps. If you had a large reserve of funds, you could have no problem buying all or most of the supply of many altcoins. With cryptocurrency, you can literally split your monetary units as small as you need them to be due to the widely varying quantities and values of the currencies which exist.

Cryptocurrency is perhaps the newest cutting edge of financial technology, so it is not surprising there is a learning curve where it takes time to understand and be comfortable with the idea. It will be seen decades from now being as revolutionary to the marketplace as actual money was when the first time man had used it instead of bartering. When

Bitcoin rolled out and entered the marketplace, it was not taken seriously by many people, myself included.

In seven years Bitcoin has come a long way from the days of being able to buy thousands of them for a mere dollar or two. Having in seven years become stable above the $1,000 mark, is truly an achievement whether or not you like Bitcoin. We are on a mission to not miss something like this again, and you can bet the next seven years will create a lot of new millionaires, perchance billionaires, and I plan that myself and as many of my readers as possible will be among those future winners.

I cannot personally eliminate poverty completely, but this is one of the best ways of doing my share to help reduce it. Do not hate money, nor the people who have it; simply divert that energy of frustration into your own endeavors and you, too, can succeed. The fact others have achieved greatly is proof that you can achieve greatly, for we all came into this world as equals, and as equals we shall go out of it. Life is too short to worry about others having what you don't. If you believe in freedom, you will understand what I am saying. The sooner you start working at getting there yourself, the longer you will have to enjoy it when you do get there, but you can't keep your eye on the prize if they are permanently stuck on other people's trophies!

The pie is not a fixed size the way so many people wrongly believe it to be, it truly grows and shrinks on its own according to what everyone collectively does in order to cause it to shrink or expand. You are not taking away from others when you are securing a share of the market for yourself, and with this kind of thing, a rising tide raises all ships. If you don't set sail, you are out of luck no matter what the tide is doing. In fact, Oliver Wendell Holmes Sr. said, "To reach a port we must sail, sometimes with the wind, and sometimes against it. But we must not drift or lie at anchor."

The Bitcoin boat has perhaps sailed out of reach to any appreciable degree if you are only interested in Bitcoin, but there is a whole altcoin flotilla out there waiting for you to hop aboard and seize your destiny by its throat. Bitcoin will break the $100,000 mark, and even the $1,000,000 barrier some day; but how many of you have $10,000.00 to buy a Bitcoin? So, if you want only Bitcoin, buy a little every month, and then listen to what I have to say in the rest of this book, so that you may multiply that wealth ahead of time. You can invest many different ways, as much or as little as you like, and still be positioned to become wealthy in a matter of years.

It took a lot for my enlightened friends to encourage me to see the light, just as it may take a lot for me to show you the light; but I am throwing everything I can at doing it. We (you and I) may be late, but we are all so early in the grand scheme; imagine if we could have been involved with the early days of banking, even the first two hundred years of banking! We are in that very position now where cryptocurrency is concerned! Imagine! We are in the first decade(s) of cryptocurrency! Think of the future potential!

It may be a foreign concept for someone who has figured out something so well for themselves wanting to share with others how to replicate their success, but yes I am really doing this because I must do this. It is one of the few things in life that by helping others you help yourself too. That is why capitalism and free enterprise are so robust and continue marching on while countless examples of communism and socialism have failed all around the world. I want to leave a legacy which parades the great prosperity which free enterprise makes possible; with a vision that champions the preservation and proliferation of real liberty.

The butcher doesn't provide meat for your dinner because he is worried you will go without food, rather he does this so that he can afford to put food on his own table by way of helping you have a source of food for yours. If all paychecks were terminated overnight, very few people would still go to work out of their altruism and benevolence. We are creatures that do things out of self-interest. It isn't selfish, it is the order of things. Only in a universe where everything exists in unlimited quantities, may this necessity of money, labor, and self-interest go away. That is how *Star Trek* portrays material gains as done away with; because if you can replicate everything in any quantity, no one will want for anything and there are no shortages. Until we meet that requirement, we cannot have a Utopia.

We must live according to our best interests because no one else has our best interests in mind, and experience has shown people who say they do, cannot be believed most of the time. The only guarantee for them to take good care of you, is if that results in your taking care of them in a mutual manner. The world would cease to function were it not for self-interest. We do not like wasting our time as a species and doing things for profit is a good use of time we could better spend doing other more important things. It is how we are able to afford to make all our dreams happen in life, leastwise the ones we are fortunate to be able to afford.

It is in my self-interest to provide you with knowledge that will benefit you. Thus incentive exists for me to bring you the best possible guide that I can. If this book and its readers succeed, I will succeed too. The more beneficial information I can put within these two covers of this book, the more valuable it will be, the more copies I will hopefully sell. Add to that, the more people who are an active part of the cryptocurrency marketplace, the more successful everyone involved will be, including those who are not yet involved. While money making secrets are usually closely guarded, not sharing what I know in this case would be counterproductive towards my own goals in life. You must have a positive effect on a lot of other people before you yourself reap a large reward.

Real security in life comes from being prepared, and leveraging every last bit of skill, knowledge, and resources you possibly can into every opportunity you are able to meet head-on. You should realize you are on a freeway of life with many exits and onramps, instead of a one-way railroad. Keep your eyes peeled for your exits, and always do something extra along the way. If you knock on enough doors, some will open, and these doors which open up can be your chance to succeed beyond what you can imagine. It does happen, it has happened, it will continue to happen. Everything you can do in addition to your routine and career will lessen your burdens in life. We only have a hundred year lease on life, and there is no harm in pursuing your dreams no matter how ambitious, when there are vehicles available which will take you there. Do not afford any room in your life for negativity and negative energy. Positive energy, positive attitudes always make for positive changes if you persist at it.

Money may not buy you happiness and it really isn't the only metric of success either, but poverty certainly does not buy happiness. If poverty bought happiness, I'd be the happiest man in the world for most of my life. Working long hours for low pay only to be heavily taxed is mere tributary slavery but we as a society are not taught how to escape this cycle. We are raised up to be "good little tributary slaves" and not look for opportunity. I have nothing against hard work, I have done a lot of hard work with nothing to show for it, and there is nothing worse than working hard for nothing. Lessening the financial burdens that we have in life is how we are able to switch from doing work we hate to pursuing the work and passions we love; the very things that we live for can become the new career choice if we secure our financial futures early enough in life.

What we love to do is usually not as profitable or lucrative as the things we hate doing are, which is why we have all done jobs we absolutely despise just to make a living. Breaking free of those burdens which hold us back from reaching our dreams should be the primary objective in life if happiness is to be achieved.

Market economics is a least liked and understood subject by so many people that concepts of money and exchange had to be explored for these people who may read this book and need caught up in order to understand just exactly why cryptocurrency is so revolutionary and important to our freedom and way of life. To understand opportunity is to unlock potential which so many people so desperately are in need of in order to reach their destiny. What they fail to see, is this potential to tap their success is within them already. Opportunities are real, but what we typically consider opportunities pale in comparison to what opportunities such as cryptocurrency can allow for us to achieve if we shall dare to involve ourselves in it.

I want everyone to understand exactly what is at stake so I will give you a few of my qualifications for writing from experience on missed opportunity. I want it burned into your mind that opportunities come and go without us even being aware of them. These are all the major opportunities I was fully aware and cognizant of; but had been powerless to do anything about them. The first two of the following examples, I want you to read, and think back over the last couple decades and answer this question: Were you aware these opportunities even existed? If the answer is no, I hope you will find your eyes have been opened. If these are the ones I knew about, what other opportunities as large or larger passed me by without me noticing?

I once knew of a $0.25 per share stock that was going to go up, no such thing as a sure thing, but that was a sure thing to me and I knew it. It was had once been a blue-chip stock, and it was a corporation well over a hundred years of age. I could not free up any of my resources to take advantage of the stock because they were locked up in a trust that was created by fraudulent means by relatives attempting to place impossible stipulations on the money such as I would never be able to fulfill leaving it to default to them, when it was to have only been a cash matter with no encumbrances originally; but in the end I was able to fight the theft and win, though the victory was as bitter as defeat. Within a year the stock headed to $2.00 a share, and within a few years it was at $10.00 a share and it even went a bit more, but by the time I freed up those funds, it was too late. That ship not only sailed, but went into orbit, too. The amount of money I would have been able to put into this stock would have been significant, and no I am not going to say what the amount was because I would rather forget. If I had a fraction of everything that rightfully was mine but I was cheated out of, I would be well off.

Then slightly later, silver was $4.00 an ounce around 2002 to 2003. I knew it was way too cheap. It is too important of a metal to be so cheap. More silver is being consumed than is mined. More short sales of silver exist than actual silver both already mined and stored above ground plus what is yet to be mined from the ground. Think about that for a minute. By the time I had any funds to spare to invest in anything, silver was already up over $10.00 an ounce and proceeded to hit about $60.00 before crashing to $30.00 and then down to about $13.00. It is stable around $17.00 an ounce right now as of November of 2017. Please, consider taking my advice and acquire some silver. Everyone I convinced to invest did well, and those who scoffed at me were not laughing when I was proven right. I knew silver was going to go crazy, and its highs are nowhere near what its real value is. Silver will do surprising things in the near future, mark my words! $200.00 an ounce is very possible for silver, and it is tangible sound money, even if it isn't legal tender like it should be, but there are people working on changing that like I said.

Yet another missed opportunity was having struck gold on the family homestead. Greedy relatives took over my great uncle's life, railroaded everything he had out from under him, and I was thrown out by them because I had all the dirt on what they were up to. There quite probably still remain thousands of ounces of gold recoverable there for someone equipped to do so and who has knowledge to do so. I know for a fact that piece of ground had never, ever, been mined to any large degree. Had these backstabbing relatives not tried so hard to get me thrown out of there, after I'd spent most of my life's free time there up to that point, I may have cut them in on the gold but no, they had to have all or nothing to sell what they ended up stealing for peanuts, and I was a threat to them getting away with what they were trying to do. I have said it before and I will say it again, blood may be thicker than water, but money is thicker than blood.

The moral of this story is that you need to do everything in your power to avail yourself to all opportunities while they are within reach, because once they are gone, it is increasingly harder to find new "sure things" that have a lot of potential for you to leverage so that you may actually succeed in your lifetime and have an honest chance at fulfilling your dreams. The larger the dreams, the more motivation you should have, because they are certainly attainable if you can convince yourself they are.

Opportunity is the most important thing for us to find in life; always guard the ones you find against anyone who would stop you from availing yourself to them. Miserable and small minded people abound, and they will always try to creep into your life and try to stand between you and your success somehow. What they can't take from you, they would destroy rather than leave it to you. Above all, never let anyone plant the seeds of doubt; any doubts you have need to be your own, and you need to do your research and critical thinking for yourself. A lot of misery exists because so many have let others do their thinking and living for them.

PART II: CRYPTO MECHANICS

Since it would be foolish and reckless for anyone to venture into any kind of opportunity without having a general knowledge and understanding of this phenomenon of Bitcoin and cryptocurrency as a whole, it was decided this chapter must be written prior to the nuts and bolts of the opportunity itself being explained. Yes, the first part of the book covered a lot of the very basics, but the purpose in this second part is to give you a well-rounded understanding of the various components which the opportunity itself revolves around.

In the interest of full disclosure, I want you to know I am not affiliated with any development of any cryptocurrency or exchange. The words "cryptocurrency", "crypto", "coin", all refer to the same thing in the context of this book and will be used interchangeably. Further, whatever coins are covered by this guide are all based on cryptographic algorithms and architecture, hence why they are called "cryptocurrency": Only those which are relevant to be used as examples or important talking points will be mentioned. I also will not recommend any coin that I myself have not mined, bought, or traded; the reason is I am very cautious about which coins I favor, and despite the hundreds which have failed and have been delisted from exchanges, I have not been involved with these "totally" failed coins. Further, it must be understood in no uncertain terms that this author is not an expert on the cryptocurrency technology itself; only the opportunity which this technology affords all of us. If you want the precise and fully detailed specifications of the blockchain for instance, go to a search engine and ask it. It is enough for our purposes to know the basics of what makes it work, and how to utilize it all.

Since this book will be on the market for many decades to come, this author further cannot guarantee any coins mentioned specifically in examples will still be around and trading by the time this pages are in your hands. Even the websites mentioned could be defunct, or rebranded on a different URL. Nevertheless, even in the historical sense, the examples should still be valuable as learning tools no matter what happens between this moment in history when this type was set (yes, it is still called typesetting even though it is digitally written) and when you actually read these words. There are thousands of cryptocurrencies, and mere hundreds will likely survive for the long run. Eventually newer editions may be published if things change substantially enough.

Let's begin with the biggest question in cryptocurrency which scares people away who are new to the whole idea: Are these currencies legal? Absolutely, although various countries have banned Bitcoin and maybe other currencies as well. Cryptocurrency is not intending to be circulated as if it were a real government issued money, so there is no counterfeiting or forgery laws coming into question on it. Bitcoin or altcoins were not created to masquerade as government issued currency. Bitcoin can only be mistaken for Bitcoin. As long as any involved parties agree to the terms of a deal or a contract, they rightfully can use anything they want as payment which is agreeable to them.

If someone agrees to pay you in gold, silver, gemstones, or even Bitcoin, there is nothing that says it can't be done. Land generally can't be used as money, simply because if you have an acre that is worth $10,000 then what happens if you want to give someone a dollar's worth of land? So that is why more practical things are used as money. However, nothing is legal tender until the Government asserts it is legal tender, meaning you can be crypto millionaire, but if you can't turn it into government greenbacks, you will not be able to use it for paying your taxes, and no one is *required* to accept it as payment. Federal reserve dollars hold the status of legal tender, because the government sanctified it as legal tender even though constitutionally it isn't; which compels everyone to accept it as such. Although gold and silver have legal tender status in many states and jurisdictions; so long as we have fiat money, our system is in direct violation of Article 1, Section 10 of the United States Constitution. Just because laws may some day pass forbidding cryptocurrency, it cannot not make something that is everyone's natural born right, into a wrong, which is to use their wealth how they see fit whatever form it is found in. We have an inalienable right to private property, and we have an inalienable right to use that property and derive benefit from it whether it is intellectual, physical, or digital.

It is just that whatever profits you make regardless of the form they are in, the IRS website makes it clear they expect you to report and pay the taxes on the fair market value of your gains, meaning to do so you would have to convert your non-money bartered items into fiat money with which to pay taxes on the fair market value gains you made from your bartering, so that you may avoid being taken down like Al Capone was, for tax evasion. Sure, you might think bartering will circumvent the IRS, but it isn't that simple. We all thought that was true at some point, because we heard other people say it, but, if you look it up you will find it right there in black and white.

The irony is, if he would have just paid the IRS their cut, there were no other crimes they could actually pin on him and he would have been a free man. That is the whole reason they used the tax laws; they wanted to get him any way they could but no other charges would stick. I only mention this because when you do become rich, I don't want you suing me for not telling you Bitcoin and your gains in cryptocurrency are taxable. When you do make a fortune, it may behoove you to have a talk with a Certified Public Accountant, just find one that isn't a crook! The federal income tax is unconstitutional, our founding fathers did not allow one, and it was not until 1913 when the elite bankers succeeded in the beginnings of taking over our money system that we were finally stuck with a federal income tax. While that is a topic for another book, you can't fight city hall, and you can't fight the IRS. Just don't end up like Al, alright?

By all means if you can find loopholes or a way around it, do what you think is right for you, but I am just trying to demonstrably show evidence that I am not at fault by not warning you adequately. That said, it is all on the honor system. None of the exchanges report to the IRS; its only if all of a sudden you start having millions of dollars in bank accounts and expensive cars and houses, you could get audited and not be very happy when they get done with you. Not having to look over your shoulders and running honest books may give you a higher quality of life despite losing so much to the tax man, and I for one feel better if I have a clear conscience, without the feeling of impending doom worrying about getting away with something. It is unfortunate that when our boat finally comes in, the IRS will beat us to the dock to help unload it. They didn't help me turn nothing into something, yet they expect a vast percentage!

This year, 2017, Bitcoin turned seven years old after having gone from perhaps a tenth of a cent per coin and even less actually, to over $8,000.00 in little over seven years. (*Over $10,000.00 now.*) Since it was first in its market, whether it failed or succeeded, these results were destined to set the stage for future attempts to create a more perfect currency that can be used for a broad range of purposes in the same way cash is used, except that cryptocurrency is created, mined, and circulated by we the people ourselves instead of by banks and governments of the world. The age old problem of the money changer still exists: No matter what the markets are doing, so long as currency is changing hands, someone is making money on those transactions and trades; but it really does not seem to be avoidable. Without the trading fees, there would be no incentive for anyone to provide these incredible exchanges. We the people have at least become our own bankers thanks to cryptocurrency, and it is the exchanges which allow commerce to function for us. Bitcoin, despite its shortcomings cannot be called a failure; it has proven to be an outstanding success not just as a technology but as a medium of exchange and a champion of liberty.

Since Bitcoin is indeed the first and most successful of all the cryptocurrencies, it has become the standard unit of exchange when valuing altcoins. You will seldom hear of altcoins expressed as being worth X amount of dollars or Y amount of any altcoin. Bitcoin is the exception to being valued in dollars. You can always view the dollar value of the altcoins on coinmarketcap.com at any time.

As money once had a gold standard, non-Bitcoin cryptocurrency very much is backed by Bitcoin even though Bitcoin is itself backed up by fiat money. Nearly all cryptocurrencies convert into Bitcoin, directly or indirectly, and it is easier to convert BTC directly into cash than the average altcoin. Few exchanges convert altcoins directly into cash balances, and not many altcoins are supported on these exchanges. It just becomes a logistical impossibility to create a be-all do-all one stop cryptocurrency exchange, so exchange owners pick and choose their battles by tailoring their offerings to the clients they aim to service.

With thousands of currencies it is impossible to have an exchange capable of changing any coin into any other coin. A few of the top coins are chosen to serve as their trading markets. This means you cannot turn Litecoin directly into

Bitcoal; So you will have to exchange the Litecoin for Bitcoin and then trade the Bitcoin into the Bitcoal. This means you are paying fees a couple of times to do one trade, but the fees are low and it is so much better than having a list that will take minutes to scroll through or even load in your browser. The typical exchanges are so resource intensive as it is that even the best smartphones have trouble allowing them to operate smoothly. There has to be a tradeoff between simplicity and complexity otherwise you will lose usability.

The exchanges themselves work just like the stock market, instead of stocks and commodities you are simply trading digital currency that is complete with tickers for each one. BTC is the ticker for Bitcoin, LTC is the ticker for Litecoin, COAL is the ticker for Bitcoal. Every altcoin has a ticker symbol that is unique. The trading works just like the stock market as there are buy and sell orders (the stock market calls them bid and ask orders, though they are the same thing and a few exchanges do in fact use those terms) which means the price goes up or down based on buying and selling activity as well as the supply and demand on each exchange for a given coin.

The difference between the buying and selling order values is what I will refer to as "spread" here on out. The spread can be very large on altcoins on a regular basis making them very lucrative for traders. Once you get the feel of a particular market, day-trading is an incredible way to build your portfolio of currencies, with the big risk being when you sell you might not be able to rebuy before it goes up and never again dropping low enough for you to rebuy. So, it is best to trade only a portion of your balance for each currency at any one time just in case something like that were to happen. Playing both sides of the spread usually works, too. What Bitcoinage you gain selling on the high side of the spread, you can place a buy order on the low end of the spread with; this will impart a gain to your altcoin balance, and your eventual total Bitcoin value of your holdings.

The process in which cryptocurrencies are initially emitted into existence, is known as "mining". Not all coins are mined; some are pre-mined and sold off in Initial Coin Offerings at a pre-determined price to speculators. Some coins sold through ICO's may well be only Proof of Stake, or even entirely pre-mined. When you hear someone say "mining" in reference to cryptocurrencies, they almost always mean "proof of work", so-called since mining rewards you for your hardware doing the work and successfully submitting the processed results to the network. There are encrypted "blocks" of data representing all of the transactions as well as the new coins to be created with that particular block plus the transaction fees accumulated for disbursement as well. The best way I can think to make this into an example would be as follows:

Let's say there is a cryptocurrency that will have twenty-five coins per block mined for a million blocks. Further, imagine each block is a bucket containing sand, with each bucket larger than the last with a bit more sand in it, with some extra rewards representing network transaction fees.

Now, the first bucket (block) is going to be very small. Imagine in the sand in each bucket, there are twenty-five small flakes of gold randomly mixed in, but you can't have any of the gold until you find them all at once, or help a group of other "miners" find them. Imagine some of the grains of sand you are sifting through represent transactions people have made while you were busy mining the last block and you are putting them where they belong as you find them.

To make that all make sense for this example, you require equipment to find the gold in those buckets, this equipment is collectively known as a "mining rig", whether it is a computer, laptop, tablet, phone, or custom built computer designed only for mining. If you are using a single computer or a smartphone to mine a cryptocurrency, it is like using tweezers to sort through all of the sand in those proverbial buckets to find the gold flakes. Not very efficient, and not very rewarding without being in on the very first buckets which are easiest to mine. A powerful graphics card would be like using a gold-pan instead of tweezers, and a massive mining rig with perhaps a dozen graphics cards working to mine cryptocurrency would be more comparable to using a giant wash-plant and a bucket loader to find those flakes of gold in each bucket.

You will not be the only miner looking for those flakes of gold, but the rule is still the same; no one gets anything until the whole block is solved resulting in all the transactions in that block being confirmed, and the coins released to either the person who's rig mined it successfully solo, or to the pool who's members collectively worked together to get the coins for themselves in which case the pool rewards them proportionally to the amount of mining power, or hash-rate as it is known, that each miner has contributed to cracking that encrypted block of transactions and rewards.

To further make the price of Bitcoin and the difficulty which it is mined make some sense; it is so hard to mine a block of Bitcoins even with the millions of computers and graphics cards and other such devices crunching away on the currency that it takes hours before a block is found. It varies, from half an hour to several hours since it is in fact random, governed by simple odds and probabilities. It would be easier for you to travel and actually find the silver dollar that George Washington threw across the Potomac, than to solo mine a block of Bitcoin.

Computer processors and even graphics processors are primarily utilized in number crunching these blocks of cryptocurrency. Specialized hardware exists which people are able to buy, such as ASICs and even FPGA's like the RaspberryPi, or Field-Programmable Gate Array. This number crunching looks for a matching "hash" which will result in a block being "mined" or "found". It isn't unlike trying combinations on a safe or combination lock until you guess the right combination, except computers are doing this countless times a second, and there are more possibilities added with each new block. Sometimes the reward values gradually decline each time a block is found, other times they halve every so many blocks as is the case with Bitcoin. When I was introduced to Bitcoin, the coins were mined in blocks of fifty coins, then the size halved to twenty-five, and they continue to halve from there on out; and yes prices doubled almost overnight with the halving from fifty to twenty-five coins a block.

The direct result of halving is the creation of a deflationary state. The markets become reluctant to sell off coinage when it is twice as hard to mine the same amount of coinage as before along with it being twice as costly, because all of the mining rigs are running on electricity. You are spending the same amount in electricity to mine half the coinage after rewards halve and this tends to have a significant impact on coin prices when compared to smooth and gradual reductions over time to the reward blocks.

There is a fixed amount of coins which will exist for a given cryptocurrency, or in cases where there is no upper limit, a simple formula governs the rate of expansion of the supply which goes on in perpetuity (forever). In either case, the coins while becoming more abundant and will also become increasingly scarce and harder to obtain over time simply because of market economics.

Over time more people will use them, more people using them means less available coins per person, and a higher value is required to encourage people who have them to sell to people who need or want them. Every retailer, every merchant who starts accepting a given coin, will add upwards pressure to the value of the coin. Bitcoin is $8,000 now because it is the most widely accepted cryptocurrency among online sellers and casinos. *(In just a few hours since updating the price in the last section, we are approaching $12K per Bitcoin now as I finish editing.)* The more successful it becomes, the more people and businesses that are going to want to adopt it, leads to a spiral upwards. While Bitcoin is in an upward spiral, the availability of Bitcoin is in a downward spiral. There are so many factors combining in a perfect storm that essentially guarantees we are going to see BTC reach the millions of dollars per coin.

Right now, .001 of a BTC is worth $12.00 give or take a few cents. When I started out with Bitcoin, a whole Bitcoin cost $2.00; we are up six thousand times in just a few short years. If you try to find anything else in the history of man which has given a 600,000% ROI in a matter of a few years, you can't find it, it does not exist. That means for every dollar you put in then, you would have made $6,000.00 at this point if you kept it all. Well ok, there are a few very ridiculous exceptions where people find a ridiculous return on investment.

There was a piece of Oak furniture at an auction house, which was heavier than even Oak should be, and Oak is heavy. When the buyer got it home, a compartment filled with gold coins was found. So yes, you can achieve a stupendous ROI in the physical real world, but you have to be insanely lucky. In cryptocurrency, you don't need luck, you just need to establish a diverse portfolio of altcoins and wait it out all while you do what you can to keep growing your investment! In other words, all you have to do is be involved and understand the opportunity that is before you! Trading, mining, working the spread between buy and sell orders.

Bitcoin was designed to require over a hundred years to mine every last new Bitcoin. The blocks that come after the last blocked mined will simply be disbursement of transaction fees collected from all of the transactions contained within the blocks; currently the fees range from hundreds of Satoshis (SATs) or thousands (KSATs) and even tens of thousands of SATs worth of fees per transaction. Consider that right now there are over a quarter of a million transactions per day on Bitcoin! That's no small amount of coinage, or dollars' worth of coinage. Bitcoin itself will only emit a total forever supply of twenty-one million Bitcoins, which while it may seem like a lot, an increasing number of them are lost forever, trapped on failed hard drives as well as lost or missing devices.

If you lose your wallet, your coins will never be recoverable which adds to the deflationary aspect of Bitcoin, for what happens when twenty of the twenty-one million Bitcoins have ended up lost and missing? You can't just call the blockchain up and say, "Hey, I lost my wallet, can you give me my coins back, please?" If you want a PC wallet that *does* let you have emergency recovery options if you suffer a total loss of your data, Armory appears to be that wallet, but it is a massive download to install it, as it has to download the core which contains the blockchain data.

It is probably important before we get too much further into this book, that I explain the breakdown of values of Bitcoin, so that you are not confused about the use of the various terms all of which in fact refer to Bitcoin and portions thereof. BTC itself is divisible down to eight decimal places. Below you can find the chart of how a Bitcoin is broken down into various "units" or specific abbreviations and terms which refer to specific divisions of a Bitcoin. The singular and plural forms are simple. If you look at the second row, it ranges from one BTM to nine-hundred and ninety-nine BTM's, for example.

BTC AMOUNT	TERMINOLOGY	ABBREVIATION
1.000 – Infinity	Bitcoin(s)	BTC(s)
.001 - .999	Bitmill(s)	BTM(s)
.00001 - .00099	KSatoshi(s)	KSAT(s)
.00000001 +	Satoshi(s)	SAT(s)

To help you understand an important part of the altcoin opportunity, the smallest price any altcoin can be when trading for BTC, is .00000001 of a BTC, or one Satoshi. This means for a Bitcoin, you can buy ten million coins if they are priced at 1 Sat. At 10 Satoshis, a Bitcoin will buy one million coins. This is very important, and will be discussed later on in full. Basically, if you can spend what now is $8,000 to buy ten million, or even one million altcoins; when they reach a dollar think about how much you've made! Coins that have traded for a few Sats have so many times reached into the BTM values. Virtually every altcoin has started out being worth mere Sats. So, let's suppose you have a million coins that you paid 10 Sats for and it goes to 1 BTM per coin. You have turned one Bitcoin into a thousand Bitcoins! So, $8,000 can turn into $8 Million.

What does this remind you of?

Yes! Penny Stocks! Oh, you could buy a thousand different penny stocks, and throw a hundred-dollar bill into each one, and chances are you won't get anywhere. On the other hand, virtually every cryptocurrency goes up, and we are talking months, rather than years of hoping and waiting. Only a few die out, only a few keep crashing. There are far more winners than losers, which makes it into the opposite of the traditional stock market. Just having coinage guarantees year after year you will gain in net-worth as denominated in BTC.

Economies of scale! The more you have of something the more valuable it can be to you! Would you rather buy one share of Berkshire Hathaway, or would you rather buy tens of thousands of shares of lesser value stocks? It is easier for a million altcoins to go from 10 Sats to 1 BTM than it is for 1 BTC to go from $8,000 to $8 Million in market value. If you have a million coins, every cent increase in market value, imparts a $10,000.00 increase to your investment. But if you had kept that Bitcoin instead of putting it into altcoins, well, every penny it increases is an extra penny you are worth. Also, just holding Bitcoin doesn't grow your Bitcoin balance, though your dollar value may go up with the BTC market. Altcoins are what you use to grow your Bitcoin balance, and Bitcoin is going up in value also, so in the end, you are gaining with two different mechanisms if you are holding altcoins.

I do want to point out that you can't "mine" shares of a company. Just one more way in which this opportunity is superior to the stock market. The cheaper a cryptocurrency is, usually the easier it is to mine more of them, and while not "profitable" to do now it is worth mining them just to have them for speculation. Speculating is far more rewarding in cryptocurrency than in just about any other venture. I was horrified just last night, 11/28/2017; the coin called UNIT, on Cryptopia, had been pumped from mere KSATs, to a peak of a whopping 75 BTMs (.075 BTC) in a few hours, then crashing back to 4KSATs! I did not have any of the currency, I never even heard of it before; so I missed out on massive amounts of wealth. There had been nearly 90 BTC worth of trade volume, and as of this moment, there is over 20 BTC of buy orders supporting the currency from crashing. So, I figure if it pumped once, it can pump again like that and I made sure to buy a decent quantity of them. If you had just a hundred coins and sold them on the peak, that's 7.5 BTC you stood to make. I am still trying to ascertain what led to that kind of a run-up, however.

Whilst Bitcoin continues to be the favorite cryptocurrency of the world, and despite the price skyrocketing for it from day to day, the greatest risk inherent with long-term investment in Bitcoin is the fact of it being so bulky of a system it could indeed collapse under its own weight as it were, or more specifically its network and transaction limitations. If the blockchain (the blockchain is an inventory system tracking every block mined and the transactions contained therein which ensures the rightful owners wallets have the proper balances at all times and that all balances are in fact legitimate) were to fail or just stop working, we are talking many billions of dollars in wealth that will not be changing hands or of any use to anyone not to mention in ten more years it could end up with a market capitalization in the trillions of dollars!

There is so much at stake, I feel there are adequate safeguards in place to deal with any contingency; there are enough hardware and software engineers involved with BTC and investing it that if there were a significant possibility of a catastrophic failure, we would not be seeing the price rise so steadily with such certainty. Diversification, though, is a great hedge. One currency may fail, but all of them certainly will not fail simultaneously.

The entire blockchain for Bitcoin as of 11/20/2017, is 142,329 Megabytes... That is 142 Gigabytes. The maximum capacity for the microSD card slot on your typical smartphone is 256 GB. The average new laptop or desktop usually comes with either a 500 GB or a 1 Terabyte (1,000 GB) hard drive. I have not had a wallet installed on my PC in years for Bitcoin, and I am not aware if they addressed this specific issue for those of us who have to download the blockchain to be able to use a PC version of their wallet. I just don't have the bandwidth and speed to cope with having to download that kind of data. But! Assuming you still have to synchronize all of the blocks in the chain still, you have perhaps months of solid downloading depending on your internet connection. Who wants to tie up an eighth or a quarter of their entire computer storage for a single cryptocurrency? And, each new block, has passed into the megabytes in size. There are of course, lite wallets which do not need the core to be downloaded in order for you to store your coins on your PC, though some lack certain features which full wallets offer.

With the increasing demand for transaction capacity, in order for the Bitcoin network to not grind to a halt they either have to increase block sizes constantly to keep up, or the fees have to increase constantly to discourage people from making unnecessary transactions. If you want your coin to boom you do not want your users to have to ration how much they use it. The whole selling point is here you have something that is so far adequate to make micro-transactions, though as of late the transaction fees easily can be more than the micro-transaction itself.

Bitcoin has so much growing left to do, that I am afraid we will not live long enough to see the blocks grow to a point at which they are never again filled to capacity. At some point you would think utilization of transaction capacity would peak, but there is no indication that is going to happen for a very long time and maybe not in our lifetimes. How many transactions do you perform in a day across all mediums? Multiply that by how many people there are: Now imagine every transaction being stored in a database. If most of the world uses Bitcoin as much as they use government issued currency now, you can understand the problem with tracking and supporting that many transactions.

At this particular moment, 11/22/2017, Bitcoin is now at $8,245.56 a coin. There are 16,694,525 mined and circulating. The market capitalization (the total value of every Bitcoin at the current market price) is $137,655,707,559. That is a hundred and thirty-seven *Billion* dollars! *(At this time of proof editing this section, it has swollen to $187 Billion!)* That is over 110 million ounces of gold in equivalent value! And it is only going to go higher! So, as you can see... If the Bitcoin developers somehow drop the ball and do not address issues before they can turn into real problems, all of that wealth can go away. The logic behind believing Bitcoin will go to millions of dollars in value, is simple: $137 Billion is such a small percentage of the entire world money supply, which is all paper save for a few jurisdictions like South Africa, where the gold Krugerrand is legal tender in addition to whatever fiat is circulated there.

Cryptocurrencies are delisted from exchanges now and then because of "corrupt blockchain" errors. I know the Bitcoin developers must have redundancies in place to prevent a corruption of their blockchain, which would be completely catastrophic; but think of all of that data that has to be kept with full integrity or this entire monstrosity can come crashing down. Cryptocurrencies are also removed for not meeting certain quotas on trade volume; i.e. no volume for a month or two would mean the coin really is dead.

Wealth created from thin air, at some point, will return to thin air and no, I am not trying to un-sell you on cryptocurrency. It may not be in our lifetimes, but certainly the Earth can't survive forever, for even our Sun someday will go nova. However, man did not make the Earth so it is not prone to cascade failures all on its own without some warning; but technology certainly is. Buildings and bridges fail, helicopters drop to the ground like rocks, but the risks are considered acceptable. Bridges do fall out from under people driving over them, but it is so rare that we accept it as safe to use these things. It is similar with cryptocurrency. Not all coins fail, and we can't afford to miss investing and leveraging a variety of them just because they might fall out from under us; there are warning signs to look for which will be discussed later.

The more pillars you have built, the stronger you will be no matter what happens, if you consider each cryptocurrency as its own pillar. Some have poor architects who are short-sighted, others are designed by geniuses in their own right. We may not always be clear on which coins were made by an idiot or not, but again there are some tips I can offer throughout the remainder of this book, notably that is why the "Good Coin Bad Coin" part is going to be included later in this publication.

Would you rather have something built by The Three Stooges? Or would you rather have something built by Frank Lloyd Wright? Of course if you want comedy, The Three Stooges are brilliant geniuses but we are not in the market for something funny right now, we need something that is built to last! In full acknowledgement and fairness to The Three Stooges, their comedy was definitely built to last and no one has come close to competing with them. They were their own breed of comedian, not to take away from others who are great in their own ways, but sometimes there are no apples to compare apples to.

Not all cryptocurrency coins are mined, there are coins that mine themselves called "proof-of-stake" (or POS), and usually the initial coins are mined in a genesis block and sold off by the developers in initial coin offerings (or ICO). POS mining is sort of like stock dividends. If you own a dividend bearing stock by a certain time(s) each year, you are paid dividends. If you have a proof-of-stake coin in your wallet untouched for the period of time specified by the developers, additional coinage will be added to your wallet based on the algorithm set by the developers of the coin, and usually you have to enable the staking feature manually which serves the purpose of indicating these coins will not be used in transactions for the foreseeable future which means to mine more coins through POS, the supply that actively circulates has to be reduced. This method of mining encourages people to hang onto their assets and not dump them into the marketplace possibly wrecking the prices.

Mined and POS coins do not make up all currencies, however. A very small portion are entirely pre-mined, that is, made to exist in their full quantity and sold off by the developers or awarded away somehow. This is a very controversial issue as some feel anyone can create a coin and attempt to sell them off essentially making instant money without offering a serious attempt at making a coin that works or does anything leaving the creators to take the money and run, while the coin dies and everyone is out their investments. If you are replacing an old coin that has failed for any reason, an entirely pre-mined currency may be just what is needed to give it a fighting chance. There are many different ways and reasons for developers choosing one method or another for the creation and distribution of their coins. There would be no point in all these currencies if they are all identical.

What about the coins that are mined? They have to be stored somehow. "Wallets" which were mentioned earlier, are simply the files on a computer, server, or any number of electronic devices capable of supporting them which serve as the containers in which cryptocurrencies are stored and are opened by software specific to that type of coin and file.

Wallet software is used for opening the wallet files containing the cryptocurrency, and enable the sending or receiving of transactions for a particular coinage; each cryptocurrency has its own unique wallet. You cannot use one wallet for multiple types of coins unless it is a specialty wallet built by a third party that is designed for use with multiple coins and only those coins which are specified. If you want to be able to store almost any coin in one place you can use exchanges for holding multiple types of coins in one mostly secure place.

CAUTION: Due to the anti-money laundering laws, and due to the Patriot Act as well as regulatory restrictions on financial institutions; you should be very cautious about housing any currency in a United States based cryptocurrency exchange. Why? Because! THIS:

The *last* thing you want to see when you go to any website, especially one with your property in any form located on it, is the above warning. It's not really a warning, because you don't get any advance notice; like Jackie Gleason said in *Smokey and*

the Bandit; "When you raid a cathouse, you take the piano player too." It is doubtful anyone's currency which was stored on that exchange will be returned to them. It has taken ten years for Liberty Dollar's to be returned to their rightful owners after the seizure NORFED went through. Bitcoin is not even ten years old! And look at the opportunity cost if you were to have to wait for ten years to get your cryptocurrency returned! A friend who used this site as early as a year ago, is very happy he got out of this exchange before he was wiped out in this seizure. Not to mention the Bitcoins seized when the "Silk Road", which used to be an online black market, was raided and shut down years ago and I recall somewhere around 180,000 BTC, based on news articles of the time, were to be auctioned off to the public after the seizure: I don't feel sorry for the Silk Road because who sends contraband through the postal service without expecting *something* to happen!

The government has to target the exchanges, because if they seize the exchange's servers, they have seized all cryptocurrency present on them. They cannot seize every computer in the country, nor can they seize cryptocurrencies without seizing the actual machines and devices they are contained on. I find my funds are much safer in other countries' exchanges who are more friendly to the cryptocurrency world. Oh, there are probably some U.S. based exchanges doing things right, but even they are vulnerable depending on which way the wind is blowing in our reactionary and progressive political climate.

You would think those crying for "separation of church and state" would not allow the government to shut down exchanges, because Jesus was the original over-thrower of the moneychangers... Well, even though that is satire, I actually am surprised being that everything is under attack these days.

Anyways, without two-factor authentication enabled, you run a high probability of being hacked and having your coins stolen with no way to retrieve them. There is no mechanism which exists to reverse any spends due to the fact these very mechanisms would be used to undermine the very purpose of cryptocurrency. Exchanges have in the past flown-by-night but with governments getting involved and requiring trading licenses, and I would assume some jurisdictions require operators to be bonded as well, it shouldn't happen much at all in the future. Some online wallets allow you to make backups of your wallet, and it is highly recommended you always keep multiple copies of your backups on different devices where only you can find them.

There are less scrupulous exchanges which abide by only those agreements they find convenient to uphold but are still happy to keep the currencies paid to them for services they refused to render as agreed. Like Abraham Lincoln said: "What kills a skunk is the publicity it gives itself." The biggest skunk I can think of is one of the largest crypto coin exchanges in the world, which has a very large, very loyal customer base, but they have no conscience when it comes to doing the right thing. C-Cex.com is this skunk I am talking about, and they 'stole' almost a Bitcoin in voting payments to list Bikercoin (BIC) to their exchange. Every week, people vote for free or with BTMs (each one counting as one vote) because the coin in first place at the end of the week's voting cycle is then added to the exchange. Of course, this was the old Bikercoin, but C-Cex still has not refunded nor acknowledged any wrongdoing. Use them if you wish, but I for one will not patronize them, because I was one of those voters burned after seeing their promises to implement the coin on their exchange if it indeed won.

If you pay to have a coin listed and they don't list it, they simply will not make it right with you. This sets the precedent for them to decide they hate your coin and you are a sucker for believing their promises. It would be understandable if they didn't state they absolutely would work on adding it if BIC won the voting, which they told many who asked and it circulated publicly for everyone involved to see, but they went back on their word. Yes, I could make some people upset by ratting them out, but, right is right and wrong is wrong, and all of us who voted for BIC gave C-Cex the better part of a year to come through for us in making things right. I owe it to you, my reader, to expose all dangers and shine a light on everything that is in my power in order that you may not fail. I could not live with myself if something I failed to warn you about cost you. I am here to help, not harm. How can you trust a site that does not stand by their promises to not run off with all of the cryptocurrencies? Even if they were to make things right, this shall stand as an example to remind everyone who is in the crypto business to do the right thing and take care of their customers.

C-Cex could have been honest in the beginning and have said that they had no intention of adding the coin, vote or no vote; but instead they baited us in and switched things around after they had the nearly an entire Bitcoin from the supporters who voted. Having a coin trading actively on C-Cex is such a big deal, we are talking a marketplace with hundreds of thousands of users! They almost are in a position to choose winners and losers. If your coin is listed there, you would have to have a terrible coin for it to still fail.

The whole point of bringing all of this to your attention is to illustrate the fact that there is no such thing as a totally safe exchange with which to entrust your cryptocurrency wealth, or expect any agreement to be honored until the moment it actually is honored. Exchanges are largely operated without regulatory oversight, which is ok in the sense we don't need government trying to make everything safe (look at all the lives ruined by the seizure as mentioned earlier, people whose wealth is inaccessible); but we do need an environment wherein exchanges can be held liable for breach of contracts. An informed user base is sufficient to hold these exchanges accountable, and the safest bet is to avoid any company or exchange that demonstrates the "customer is never right" attitude. I just wish a working, reputable, escrow system was devised in order that anyone could sell anything to anyone with complete peace of mind that the purchased items would arrive without the paid currencies being stolen.

There are plenty of exchanges that treat their customers with great respect and do not exploit them, www.cryptopia.co.nz/Register?referrer=meinkoin has operated as a prime example thus far of what a fair and honest exchange looks like, and I will endorse them for the foreseeable future.

(I provided the whole referral link if you don't mind typing it in when you register; the 10% of trade commissions I would earn is insignificant because fees are so small here to trade; but it is valuable information for me to visualize how much impact this book is actually having on my audience by seeing how many referrals I actually gain. If you do not want to use my referral link, that is ok; it just means I have no way to gauge the effectiveness of mentioning specific things in a book such as this, and Cryptopia will receive 100% of all trade fees. On the up-side, it is not multi-level, and you can refer people for yourself too! It is free to register, no fees, except on currency exchanges.)

Nothing is unreasonable about how Cryptopia treats their customers especially when there is a customer support issue, except now as Bitcoin prices go up, so do their withdraw fees to pull Bitcoin out of their exchange. It started out at .001 of a BTC, which was fine, but in recent weeks it went to .002 of a BTC which we are now talking $22.00 to make a withdrawal! The rest of the hundreds of altcoins there are cheap to withdraw still. And they do operate a marketplace that has no fees for buying and selling, so at least we do get our money's worth out of them. The fees for trading are very small as well. So, you see, I can live with that. The Bitcoin network varies your fees for transactions relative to how long you are willing to wait for them to find room to pack your transaction into a block. A few hundred SATs in fees could have you waiting days for it to go through; right now if you want priority transactions, the actual fees are around 1.5 BTMs or .0015 of a BTC, so it isn't Cryptopia's fault for the high fee. Generally, when people do take coinage out it is because they are needing it as soon as possible.

Online wallets and exchanges operated by the official developers of cryptocurrencies for their own cryptocurrencies, are the exception. These wallets are usually integrated into the same platform as their version of the blockchain, and while these are not generally exchanges, they do exist as a combination such as Cryptopia for instance. Their exchange is powered by their own currency, called the DOT: Payment in the form of DOTs is what they charge to add your coins to their exchange. Even the referral commissions are paid in DOTs even though people can buy and sell and transact business with DOTs too. If you are going to make your own currency, what better way than to build whole platform for it to be used on right out of the box!

As for the safe online storage of digital currency, the official websites of the project itself that are home to the blockchain, are not likely to go away. Bitcoin can be stored online at blockchain.info, since they support online wallets and are as official as you are going to get. The day your wallet and coins are inaccessible on that website, is the day Bitcoin is dead, and no one anywhere will be using any wallet or Bitcoins until it is running again, so complete safety only comes from the people and organizations actually responsible for seeing to the ongoing operation of a coin.

The rule of thumb for limiting your risk is to only keep as much coinage stored in an exchange as is necessary to facilitate trading or any other activities you are engaged in with them. It becomes complicated trying to store many different cryptocurrencies on your own computer, but unfortunately it can be necessary if you are in it for the long term. If you don't possess it and can't hold it, you don't own it; well, the closest you can get to this is keeping your wallets and coins on your own computer or other devices when they are not needed to be kept in exchanges. In my own direct experience, everything kept on the "cloud" as it is now known, is a mistake. What is on the cloud eventually becomes irretrievable at some point. We forget usernames and passwords, or we get hacked and completely lose access and I tend to trust myself and my computers more than I trust someone else's.

"Physical" wallets exist, but they are useless if you do not have electronics and internet access with which to utilize them again. They are merely physical tokens which without technology and internet, the coinage they represent cannot be redeemed or accessed. There is no way which I know of to reliably transfer cryptocurrency through physical means without the aid of electronics to verify the coins really are loaded on that physical wallet whether it be metal or paper.

Sure "coins" representative of the currency they are "loaded" with can be handed off to another person as a payment method, but without access to the internet how can you prove to someone the valuable portion, which is the cryptocurrency, is actually on it?

I have seen exchanges that let you print out paper "vouchers" which would be good for the amount of cryptocurrency paid into the server for printing it out specified on the document; the problem is what happens when the servers go offline or the exchange shuts down? You are stuck holding worthless paper. Cryptocurrencies continue to live on and for the most part they cannot be shut down, even dead coins are still technically "alive"; the mechanism with which to retrieve the coins backing up a voucher of any kind is not so certain to endure the test of time and regulation changes.

The exception to paper wallets are found in the paper-wallet backups which are printable from PC based wallets such as Armory Bitcoin wallet. You can actually recover a lost or missing wallet in Armory as long as you have the paper-based backup of your wallet should you have printed it out or saved a scan of it somewhere safe. You can never keep enough copies on enough different mediums of your wallets and their backups. Avail yourself to every possible recovery method in the event the worst does happen; you do not want to be wiped out needlessly.

To further aid you in limiting risk, beware of the old coins being shut down (removed from exchanges, essentially dying) to bugs or other problems and conversion programs being announced following these failures supposedly offering a "solution". Do not believe any conversion program that is not announced in the developers own newsletters, forum posts from the official developers, or on the official website of the coin. There is nothing to keep someone from beating the developers to the punch by fearmongering the coin owners into believing they are at risk for missing a very short deadline for turning in the old coins for the new replacement coin; by the time the fraud is discovered, you've had your coins stolen before the official conversion takes place leaving the scammer to redeem your coins for themselves. You will always want to make absolutely certain such conversions are legit before participating as coins once sent are irretrievable. Even in the case of the old Bikercoin, there is nothing to say the official conversion wasn't a scam.

If we give up the old coins for new coins on a new platform, who is to say someone will not patch the old Bikercoin and it will be valuable again leaving the developer to sell all the old coins once they are fixed? You must always do extensive research and verify everything before you jump in with both feet, where your wealth is concerned. I never witnessed nor was I ever able to reproduce the alleged "counterfeiting coins" glitch responsible for killing most of these cryptonote currencies; did it even exist or was it just a ploy? I cannot say for certain. What I do know, is the surviving cryptonote currencies such as XMR and COAL have upgraded to the patched version of software in which this vulnerability was removed.

Since cryptocurrency is a lot like the stock market, you may be wondering if there are indexes for tracking these currencies. Yes, there actually is an index of cryptocurrencies, though details on how to use it to your advantage in pursuing the opportunity this book is centered around, will be provided in later chapters. Coinmarketcap.com is the essential index of cryptocurrencies acting as a sort of research directory. It is the "Who's Who" of cryptocurrency. If a coin doesn't get listed there, it is going to have a hard time being taken seriously among the cryptocurrency community. New coins require significant milestones to be reached by any cryptocurrency before Coinmarketcap will even consider accepting their application for addition to the site; any old coin which is not yet on this site likely isn't one to take seriously, and investors generally do not take them seriously.

Not only does this site collect and display data on trade volume and current prices, but it provides charts and the number of coins currently in circulation. Links pertinent to the coin you are researching are provided also on the listings for each coin so that you can do further research, and even learn how to mine them or where to exchange for them. Sometimes the pages are out of date with regard to links and available information, but they usually rely on users to report updates and changes to the listings. Normally the lower total supply of a coin that is to exist means the higher the potential value will be. If there are hundreds of billions, trillions, or more of a particular coin slated to be mined it is to be treated as a scam coin.

Forums do exist in abundance, but you have a lot of opinion and bias to sift through in order to gather the information and facts which are actually useful to you. There is nothing which exists, real or imagined, that has absolutely no haters hating it, especially where cryptocurrency is concerned. Water has enemies; there are people who hate water so much they would rather spend the remainder of their lives on dialysis than drink water, some of whom I've personally known. It is to be said, even amidst the consequences of their stubbornness, they were at least true to themselves unto the bitter end, but at a hell of a cost.

There are a lot of naysayers and pessimists who are ready to shoot down even the best idea just because they don't like it or think it is inferior to their own projects. If you have a problem getting something to work right with your wallets or mining software, the forums will have the answers most of the time. I have not yet seen any cryptocurrency which does not have its own proprietary website complete with information and software necessary to use the coin. If possible it is best to gather your information for big decisions from proprietary sources, such as the developer's own forums, blogs, or websites. Third party sources are notoriously unreliable.

The best time to get in on a currency is when it is freshly launched, with coins often starting to trade at a single Satoshi each, usually going higher fairly quickly as time passes, with mining growing more difficult from week to week. It is worth mining mountains of coins in these early days just because all you are out is a little time if they do not amount to anything. More often than not they do get listed, and you are able to cash in on them eventually making it the cheapest most cost effective way to speculate. The announcements for brand new coins launching usually take place over the forums so it is best to try to keep your ears to the ground now and then, and your eyes peeled for news and advertisements .

The chief difference between cryptocurrency and let's say, a digitally circulated dollar, is that a dollar can be charged back in the case of fraud or theft. Cryptocurrency cannot under any circumstance have a transaction reversed, so you must be very aware of what is going on and safeguard them to your utmost ability. Once you pay for a product or service, that's it, you have no guarantee of delivery of the product or service and while escrows have operated successfully in the past, they ultimately have been destroyed by regulations requiring escrow licenses. It is funny that the regulatory agencies are destroying the very thing that would prevent the need for regulations because they do not comply with existing regulations. Government is one massive paradox and almost always work against the best interests of the people which it exists to protect and serve.

I understand a lot of things still may not make sense even after reading this far, but I won't leave you hanging. This is such a massive topic to cover, and there are so many more pages which will come after the end of this section. I had to learn myself by jumping into this world of cryptocurrency without knowing whether I could swim or not, and without a flotation device too! That is, there wasn't much of a guide for me at all in those days, and all of this I currently bring to you is out of my firsthand experience and knowledge from many countless hours spent researching and making decisions on which way to go.

There is very little general knowledge regarding cryptocurrency amongst the general population since, up until recently with Bitcoin hitting all the news outlets from breaking record prices, no one ever talked about it to the point of it being as common to hear about such as sports are, or the weather. As that gap closes, cryptocurrency prices are going to go leaps and bounds beyond what they are now; it is something called the "S-Curve" in economics. As an idea or a product reaches a certain market saturation slowly, once it hits that magic number, I think around 5%, it explodes and goes so viral, in a short time market saturation will rise to over 50%. Meaning instead of one in twenty people knowing about something or using it, more than one in two people will have bought into it. This point at which the slow growth stops and the booming growth begins, is called "critical mass". If someone tells you something is going to go critical, this concept is likely what they are referring to.

There are many signs of cryptocurrency being at, or at least being very nearly upon that magical point of critical mass. A large percentage of posts in my feed from friends who never posted about cryptocurrency, are now asking about Bitcoin or some other such coin. You hear about them on the radio, you see them mentioned on TV, or hear them talked about on the radio. This motivated me to actually finish this project, because every delay is costly not only for my future reader, but for me in that every day this book is not finished, is a day I am not selling it. Every day there are altcoins doubling and tripling in price; you are missing out on all of them which have done so and I do not want you missing out on these astounding gains on the ones which will do so again in the future!

I want to see everyone excited about this opportunity which is currently before every person on the planet who has internet and a computer, or a smartphone; but for everyone not just to be excited about it or know about it. Everyone can, and should do something about it! This opportunity is life-changing, and we can build a better society with the successes we make here in cryptocurrency. Our dreams, our ambitions, all become within reach for those who dare to learn, and avail themselves to this path. If you want to eliminate poverty, this certainly can eliminate yours and mine, and anyone else's hands we can put a copy of this book into! You only have to apply yourself, and motivate yourself.

There are many different things you can do to get where you are going in life, but it isn't acceptable to just give up and say to yourself, "I will continue to be stuck at my job the rest of my life and my dreams do not matter because I will never be able to afford them." Giving up is not an option, and there is no need to give up. If there is one thing we can learn from President Nixon, it is precisely that; you are not ruined until you resign yourself from the idea of success. Opportunity is everywhere, and everyone who has made their success and fulfilled their dreams and ambitions has at some point in their lives realized this.

If Thomas Edison would have stopped inventing the lightbulb a few hundred failures into trying to create it, we would have been using kerosene lanterns a lot longer than we had to. After electricity was harnessed and lightbulbs invented, Nikola Tesla won the contract to light the World's Fair which show-cased the new electricity age; but Edison would not let him use his lightbulb designs as they were patented and the two were *not* friends. They were such bitter rivals, that Edison used Tesla's Alternating Current (which is what our whole grid runs on because it is more efficient than Edison's Direct Current) to electrocute animals as a way to try to scare people from adopting the Alternating Current; among the animals Edison electrocuted, was an Elephant. *(If you want to read about it yourself, here it is, even a clip from the film Edison himself had recorded of the event: https://www.wired.com/2008/01/dayintech-0104/)*

Tesla did not give up, and Edison probably expected the contract to be abandoned since he owned the lightbulb patents; how could Tesla come up with hundreds of thousands of lightbulbs of a new design which didn't infringe on the patents? Tesla responded to this challenge by inventing his own Tesla base lightbulb; this lightbulb Tesla created in order not to violate Edison's patent lives on even now as the "Christmas Tree lightbulb." Yes, the same infuriating ones which if you have one burned out bulb you have to go through each and every one until you find the right one to replace for the whole strand to work again!

The faster you fail, the sooner you will find success. Sometimes you have to say you can, and build your wings on the way down after you have jumped into it. Success will always eventually happen no matter what niche you are trying to conquer. This is why motivational speakers make vast fortunes from speaking and motivating people, because making people determined and resolved to succeed is what keeps the world turning. You cannot motivate people if you cannot convince them there is hope, and unmotivated people do not achieve anything great in life. Life is hell, not for everyone certainly, but even the people with the best of lives can have the worst of days, and the toughest of challenges. You can sit on the sidelines and mope about how unfair life is, how big your failures are, or you can empower yourself to make changes happen.

The whole reason I am an author, is because I had to cross that bridge myself and I've made a lot of differences for a lot of people. Reading reviews on my books and seeing that my prospecting book helped someone find their first flake of gold for the first time makes me feel better than hitting any jackpot or having any amount of money. You see, gold prospecting really is the most rewarding outdoor activity one can experience. If you never find anything, you've still found nature, fresh air, and better health; and have connected yourself to one of our greatest heritages. My philosophy is fairly simple: If I end up helping even one person have a better life after they read the pages contained within this book, or any I have written, it was worth writing.

I wasn't born into money; I am self-made but I've got a lot left to accomplish before I am what I would consider a real success. I don't want to be anything but self-made, because I don't like owing anyone anything; especially my time. If you have a career, you owe the boss your time. It has been said not to squander time, for that is the stuff life is made of. It has also been said that time is the fire in which we burn, so let's get on with it, shall we?

This opportunity in cryptocurrency is not something that only a few can succeed at, this is something everyone can succeed at. You do not even have to be out of high school to begin! If you play computer games, you have everything you need to start out mining cryptocurrency. Let your computer work for you while you go to school! Don't get in a hurry to sell your mined coins either, unless you are trading them to make more. If you put some of your allowance and Christmas money into hardware for mining currencies, it is that fewer years you will have to work at MacDonald's to pay your way through college, or to pay for college afterwards with when you find out there are no jobs for the degree you signed away your life to buy. College has descended to such a disreputable state, that it very much is a criminal enterprise, and the government is running a protection racket for them. You can't go bankrupt on federal student loans; and your income taxes and wages can be garnished especially if you are working and barely surviving with no way to afford repaying them! Even if you were totally scammed and ripped off like I was! So, just be careful, don't get in a hurry to do something so costly just because everyone you know is pressuring you to do so. College is not the future, it is the past, and you should only do something so costly if you have a rock solid plan and know exactly where it is going to lead you. That is my advice to any youth reading this book.

Not everyone can make a good living being a car salesman. Not everyone can go to work in a restaurant and make a fortune in tips. Certain things require you to be a people person to do well at. Not all of us are people persons, and not all of us are comfortable doing things that we probably would do well at if we had to do them. Stress is unhealthy, so it's best to avoid the things that are miserable for us to do. Cryptocurrency shatters the entire social construct of traditional opportunity. There is nothing to sell here, nothing to buy, you can do it your own way on your own terms. Introverts, extraverts, confident and insecure people all can find their success here in cryptocurrency. It doesn't matter what you believe, it doesn't matter what you think; cryptocurrency opportunity is real without regard to any metric, and it is not going away. There are simply too many things for that the things against it have little effect to slow it.

Just as we were born too late to get in on the gold rushes of yesteryear and we did not miss out on gold completely; we have not missed out on Bitcoin or the competing currencies which have sprung forth in the wake of its tremendous success. The old-timers did not find all the gold; and the cryptocurrency rush is still in full swing!

If you say you are looking for gold, the scoffers who bought into the lie that the old-timers mined all the gold say we are crazy! Who is crazier? The person who has in recent years mined two ounces of gold in one day with a shovel and a sluice, or the person who believes it isn't out there to find? Just as people will say we are crazy when we tell them that cryptocurrency is going to make us wealthy! Who's laughing at who? A year ago a friend told me Bitcoin will never go to $5,000, or $10,000 and here we are! Just the other day I took a whole BTC of trading profit when I sold altcoins on a high streak.

Looking for wealth in any form gets us ridiculed and laughed at, but the joke is on them. There is a lot of gold still out there, probably even near where you live and you don't even know it. Just as the ability to build a massive holding of cryptocurrency is at everyone's fingertips. I guarantee you in all of the time you've spent outdoors, you've been walking on top of millions in gold at one time or another. Sure, sometimes it is silver, but it all spends the same if you will just avail yourself to finding it despite what people are telling you!

Bitcoin is a similar deal. Sure, we may be a bit late to get in on the original BTC rush, but there is a whole lot of opportunity to extract Bitcoin from the altcoin rush! There are opportunities right now, that if you mine or buy any number of different currencies, you can make millions! Even though there are many people who will say "you will never make millions at anything." You know what? A million dollars is *only* a thousand thousands. How many piles of a thousand dollars have passed through your hands and you aren't a millionaire yet and neither are they? Scary isn't it. Yet here we are, and with what to show for it?

When you've reached the end of the book, it should all fall into focus, and you will be well prepared for your journey down this path, or just about any. Timeless principles are central to any opportunity; this just happens to be the perfect subject to present them to you in.

Achieving your largest of dreams quite literally could be a few years away, or sooner, depending on how you leverage your way through with everything you are going to learn. The point is that we can all get there if we allow ourselves to realize anyone can do it, and that literally anyone has done it so far. Success in Bitcoin has not been exclusive to one class of people or one culture of people. It is not exclusive to any ideology. It is derived from the one common thread every person was born with; the desire for freedom and liberty. All people in all countries in all ways of life have been propelled to new heights in prosperity, simply because they availed themselves to what opportunity lay before them in cryptocurrency especially when there literally are no other opportunities in some corners of the world.

It isn't that everyone missed out because they wanted to; but a large number of people simply had no clue of the tremendous opportunity which Bitcoin and all of the altcoins to follow it would provide. In 2011, you couldn't have run up to random strangers to offer them Bitcoin with the line of, "Hey, buy these because they are going to be worth $10,000.00 in less than a decade." No one would have believed it then. Only a very few who were in on the vision from the beginning had that kind of foresight to think that way. To 99.999% of the population, Bitcoin was only just a novelty, a digital trinket, like those glass beads people traded to natives for truly valuable stuff.

The intent of this book is to prevent this from happening to us over and over again as time goes by, no matter what the next big thing is to come our way. At the very least, if you do decide not to pursue cryptocurrency; consider the principles I am giving you throughout this book. These principles easily can be applied to any number of other opportunities. Really, opportunity itself is what is important. We are only defeated if we stop searching, and stop trying; but as far as Cryptocurrency goes, there is nothing else on Earth quite like it.

PART III: GOOD COIN - BAD COIN

Before jumping into mining, buying, or selling and trading cryptocurrencies, the first thing for you is to learn how to research and consequently become familiar with the various coins out there for the purpose of discerning the good coins from the bad ones. A good coin can make you prosper, but going into a bad coin, especially at the wrong time, can be devastating. Self-interest is very much alive and the creators of each of the coins out there understand the mechanics behind their coin and how to use it for their benefit. For that matter, coins have been created which are intended only to benefit the developers themselves and a lot of people have been burned by "scam coins". Figuring out what the future holds for any given cryptocurrency goes a long way towards us looking after and securing our own best interests.

The time you will spend mining a bad coin can never be recovered, though financially you aren't out much; all the while the good coins have become harder to mine in the time spent mining a bad coin, which is the hidden opportunity cost. If you are buying your way into a portfolio, it is best to buy into a coin that won't disappear soon after you bought it. If you are mining your portfolio and not buying into any coins, choose a handful that you wish to obtain, and rotate your mining through them until you are satisfied with your results or until those coins you have chosen become too difficult and expensive to mine efficiently.

Naturally everyone thinks 'their' coin is the 'best' coin and it is easy to get caught up in the hype as well as the pompously arrogant attitudes prevalent amongst the various cryptocurrencies and their user bases. Many "coin communities" are almost entirely composed of good people, and it is why I respect those coins in particular. The group of people centered around a particular coin really is like a community due to certain temperaments congregating around certain coins more than others. This is not a bad thing, but you have to beware of unfounded since it will only cloak the actual risks and maybe even hide the actual potential value from you. You want to ignore the opinions and focus on the realities of which there are certain ones that will govern all coins as universal principles which are the primary ones to be concerned with. That is the goal for this part of the book.

Scarcity is our first stop; it is that quality which gives all things found in life actual value. Limited supplies of everything to supply unlimited needs and wants. It is the idea that everything no matter how abundant or rare, has a limited quantity which does and will ever exist so therefore it has some kind of a value depending on how useful it is and how much demand there is for it. The reason paper money eventually becomes worthless is that it has only an arbitrary limit which historically was regulated by the speed at which the printing presses can pump out money. If you run low on paper and ink, there's still no limit to how high of a denomination you can put on a piece of paper. While governments can decree more paper money, they can't conjure gold and silver to exist out of thin air in the same way, hence why commodity money is the guardian of wealth and purchasing power, and why governments were so eager to destroy those standards of backing money with metal.

Cryptocurrencies tend to have some real limit placed on their expansion and quantities to be mined. While they have no intrinsic nor indestructible value, so long as they are useful, this limit will impart value to the coin. You are going to need a coin that is secure from being counterfeited in any way, or falling victim to any other exploit. With the "counterfeiting" bug found in the Cryptonote currencies, and with double-spend exploits being old news and met with various countermeasures and fail-safes, there isn't a lot to worry about, generally speaking. Developers usually are proactive in shutting down any bugs or exploits before they become a problem.

The more coins which will exist, the less value they can be expected to hold though some cryptocurrencies are shocking in that while they are as plentiful as grains of sand on a beach they seem to defy this rule and go quite high in value. The bottom could fall out from under such abundant coins at any time. Even if an abundant coin becomes very popular and useful, it will not become worth as much as it would if there were fewer of that coin issued. Imagine if every person in this world had exactly one million dollars; do you think a dollar would buy much? No! It wouldn't. Money would be equally worthless were it distributed equally and in great abundance. Only after it becomes unevenly and very widely distributed does currency gain value. Such is the reality also with cryptocurrencies.

A good coin will be limited to anywhere from a few thousand to a few hundred million coins. Any coin that is to be mined into the billions or trillions, is considered a scam coin. The reason being is that if you make a brand new coin with a trillion of them to be mined in a short period of time, the market cap of that eventual supply is an astounding 10,000 BTC at the lowest possible market price of one Satoshi or 0.00000001 of a BTC per coin. That's $100 million dollars at present values (Nov. 2017), created out of thin air immediately with no past history or reputation established. The *only* reason people even pay one Satoshi a coin is due to the fact you can't divide a BTC any further than one Satoshi. People who do buy it are only hoping for it to go to two, or three satoshis so they can double or triple their money and sell out. And what if 25% of the coins are pre-mined? That would give the developers more than $25 million dollars just for creating it! They would dump all their pre-mine and take your money and run all the way to the bank laughing until they drowned in their own tears!

At a time when a friend of mine had been mining DCY (Dinasty Coin) to the tune of several million coins a day, the developers of the coin were going around to exchanges trying to get administrators of the exchanges to fix the price of their coin to at least several euros each. Further, they were trying to sell the wallet (wallets are entirely free for all serious and legitimate coins) for an astonishing amount on the order of a hundred-and-fifty Euros! I personally found craigslist ads whereby they were trying to sell DCY for ten euros each; a coin that is as scarce as grains of sand are on a beach and worth less than a grain of sand is worth!

DCY is so abundant that it is already overpriced at one satoshi, yet it was up to fifty satoshis this year (2017) on Cryptopia, but has crashed since. It is trading between five and twenty Sats currently based on recent history.

As of this writing, there are over 1.42 Billion DCY mined into existence, and they are trading at seven Satoshis a coin! In order for them to actually be worth the ten Euros a coin the creators tried desperately to rig the markets to on them, that's *fourteen billion Euros* of market cap which they were trying to invent when it is actually only $910,000 in fair market value, that is to say what investors actually say they are worth on the free market! Such an abundant coin cannot ever realistically become worth a tenth of the entire Bitcoin market! Always investigate all claims and be familiar with the supply of the coin, and market conditions which will impact the value of the coin. Anyone who did pay ten Euros for a

DCY is likely not very happy right now. Oh, someday they may be worth ten Euros, but only because Bitcoin will keep going to the moon. If Bitcoin goes high enough, a single Satoshi may eventually be worth that much, meaning every coin is worth not less than that much, also! I am not saying to never buy DCY or use it; but do not forget *caveat emptor*.

Are grains of sand rare? No, of course not. Can you count them? No. Is there a finite supply of sand? Yes. Would you buy a grain of sand for ten Euros? No! Unless it happens to be a diamond or a gold nugget! This very same reasoning applies to cryptocurrencies. To be clear, there is more than one type of sand in the world and some are extremely rare and valuable with most being fairly common and ordinary.

Some people look at new coins and think, "not another coin"; but competition is good and the best coins quickly rise to the top in the crypto world. There are a lot of excellent coins that are just slow to gain attention and be taken as the serious contenders which they truly are. This delay in markets correcting themselves, leads to one mechanism enabling this opportunity to exist for us. It gives us a chance to prepare.

If you look at the successful and valuable currencies, Bitcoin is limited to twenty-one million coins, estimated to be completely mined around 2140. It is a lot of coins, but demand is such that it supports a $7,500-$12,000 market price currently with about 16.7 million coins mined so far. Keep in mind, while it sounds like a lot of coins, there are well over 300,000,000 people living in the United States, this means the current supply already mined thus far is about 0.055 of a Bitcoin existing for every American man, woman, and child. If you consider we are fast approaching seven billion people in the world, if it hasn't already been surpassed, there only exists a little over 0.002 of a bitcoin for every man woman and child. This is scarcity at its best and would ensure a high market value should Bitcoin's popularity and usage begin to rival that of fiat money to any large percentage. At some future date, it is foreseeable that holding any amount of Bitcoinage at all could make a person wealthy but you do not grow your portfolio by simply holding onto it; you grow it by knowing what to do with it. Or, you can treat it like a retirement fund and toss amounts into it regularly to keep your balance climbing. Cashing in on the altcoin opportunity is the fastest and cheapest way to grow your Bitcoin assets. People still mine Bitcoin, but with the same amount of investment in hardware, you can mine far more Bitcoin by mining altcoins.

The first characteristic to look for in picking a good coin is to see that there is not an excessive amount of coins to be created, and if there is a large quantity to be mined that there isn't a large amount of pre-mined currency which would make the developers the big winner rather than the miners themselves. The exception is of course when a coin is entirely pre-mined, such as the new Bikercoin was. *(I do not endorse the new BIKER coin; it is unclear if the developer will ever do anything to cultivate the market. It is very speculative now.)*

If you think having a few billion coins existing and trading is ridiculous; I stumbled across the most horrible scam coin ever: Dentacoin (DCN) currently has 325 Billion mined coins, with a supply limit of 8 Trillion coins! Think about that for a minute and let it sink in. The value of holding cryptocurrency is in being able to convert it into money or Bitcoin when you need to; there are so many DCN for sale right now, that there are no buy orders for these coin holders to dump to. It would take 9 BTC in buy orders just to push the coin into the 2 SATs of value. No one is going to put $100,000 into a 1 SAT coin that is this abundant! COAL is limited to 12.5 Million coins, and I was buying them between five and ten Satoshis back in the beginning! Massive difference! And COAL has stabilized around 300 Satoshis as of November, 2017. Low values are fine if the coin has a rather limited supply.

A good coin does not charge its users a fee just to have the wallet or to store coins whether you use them or not; Dinasty Coin tried selling their wallet to their users for a whopping one-hundred and fifty Euros! I personally ran across this when

I first looked into DCY. I was going to mine a few just in the odd chance they became worth anything at all before they did become listed on an exchange. The only fees incurred by an honest cryptocurrency are the transaction fees: When you send cryptocurrency, a very small amount is charged which is credited to the block that when mined, the fee goes to the miners in addition to the normal block reward. In a few instances, there are coins where the developers take a cut of the transaction fees for maintenance of the project with a majority going to the miners.

Important indicators as to how solid a coin is for our purposes, is to ask the following questions: Is there a dedicated and qualified development team? Is there a loyal and active fan-base? Is there continual discussion on moving the coin to the next level and promoting it throughout the market place? If none of these exist, then you will want to examine the trade volumes for the coin on whatever exchanges have it listed. Many exchanges de-list currencies if the trade volume falls below a certain amount for a certain period of time as denominated in BTC value.

Is the coin actually used now? If so, what is it used for? Some coins exist to be utilized in commerce, others are built entirely with the intention to be used as money for games. This enables real wealth to be used in gaming, and can be the currency used for buying upgrades, or any component key to the game itself which chooses to utilize it.

Bitcoin, and Litecoin are general purpose coins, used in all forms of commerce, gaming, and trade. There are actually Bitcoin ATM machines in existence allowing you to buy Bitcoin as you need it, or even sell it, but I do not hear much of them appearing in the United States although they seem to have caught on in Europe.

Ethereum is a bit more advanced than the traditional cryptocurrency, in that it is not just a currency but an entire platform which enables smart contracts to be utilized. People can create their own "tokens" or "coins" which operate on the back of the Ethereum platform. It is still something I have not been involved with to any appreciable degree, but once this book is done maybe I will try to master the world of Ethereum, and publish another book dealing entirely with that aspect of cryptocurrency. The moment I saw that it was a whole entire platform that people could do their own thing with, it is kind of mind-blowing. It means there is infinite potential for value because there are potentially limitless uses for it.

The major selling points for cryptocurrency in the old days centered around the "anonymity" factor. Bitcoin was hailed as the perfect internet cash upon its entry to the world stage. Everyone had been told and were led to believe it could not be traced, and transactions were made with impunity until it came time for crimes to be prosecuted using the fact Bitcoin is traceable. This resulted in altcoins being created to address the issue. Monero (XMR) is the real deal for anonymity along with other currencies built on the cryptonote or cryptonight algorithm. Truly untraceable and anonymous transactions are why Monero has been trading between ten and thirty BTM's and could someday rise much higher; Bitcoal also operates on this algorithm, and it has the potential to catch up to, and even surpass Monero. *(Interestingly, with the same mining rig, on an average day at this moment, despite the difference in price between COAL and Monero; they generate the same BTC value of coinage when mined. Mining difficulty seems to be the basis coins are valuated against.)*

Bitcoin responded to the privacy and anonymity issues by devising one time use addresses. Every transaction is performed under a new wallet address that is randomly generated. Some see this as a half-baked attempt to solve the problem, but it comes down to one thing: If you absolutely need privacy, it is best to utilize currencies which were designed specifically for privacy and anonymity.

Then, you have Ethereum. I am not at all familiar with how it rates in the whole privacy and security arena. In fact, I missed the Ethereum boat because there were so many more Ethereum than BTC and I thought why would Ethereum be worth anything? Naturally, I didn't bother to learn the whole story of Ethereum, in that it was actually an entire platform. When I say platform, I mean it in the same way that a workbench with tools is a platform; a platform that lets you build and do things that you want to do, and add functionality to various things. Had I known that it wasn't just another coin, sure, I probably would have invested. It offers so much more than just the ability to make transactions and provide a unit of accounting. For one thing, there was no one to tell me about it, at least you are aware of enough now that you can research it if it interests you. I didn't even know it was worth researching, which had resulted in a very costly lack of knowledge for me. Ethereum started out in the KSATs, and proceeded to grow into the 80 BTM range, but has since backed off to about 40 BTMs.

Another defining quality as to a coin's being good or bad, is how fast transactions are and how cost effective and efficient a given coin is to use. Bitcoin can take one or two hours to confirm a transaction. Several blocks (each new block after a transaction is made, is called a confirmation because it validates spends) are required to be mined before the typical merchant clears your purchase or deposits into your accounts.

These multiple confirmations are usually required to ensure someone did not exploit the system, and double spend the coins, or any number of other possibilities. You can envision a double spend by looking back in time. Remember when people would tape a string to a coin, put it in a vending machine and pull the coin back out yet still get what they "bought"? Yes, that is basically what the double-spenders accomplish, and it is the merchant that suffers from the activity. Confirmations make sure the coins that you spend or receive are legitimate coins and that they won't disappear from your wallet after a confirmation does come in.

Can you imagine paying at the fuel pump with Bitcoin at a

gas station only to have to wait for one or two confirmations before you can drive off? It would be ridiculous to have to wait an hour or two before being allowed to leave! Maybe there is some way of making exceptions in such an instance; however, it doesn't matter where you use your cryptocurrency, waiting an hour or two for the balance to be accessible is just maddening, and a rather large inconvenience. This is just one of the reasons Bitcoin may not be *the* best cryptocurrency.

By this metric, Bitcoin is not a very good coin, yet it is the proprietor of cryptocurrency and is considered amongst the best. A coin that has nearly instant confirmations will go far, especially if it improves on security and privacy at the same time. I would say anywhere from thirty-seconds to five-minutes is acceptable for a coin that is considered "fast". Any coin which doesn't end up with an overloaded and plugged up network because of heavy utilization, stands a chance at climbing the charts towards greatness. Any coin that will take longer than Bitcoin to confirm, might as well be considered dead on arrival. People just do not want to have to wait.

It is silly having to wait on money that is electronic and digital in this computer age. The exception is the specialty niche coins, whose use may not necessitate or be dependent upon a fast confirmation time and where it is ok if a significant confirmation period elapses. If a currency is designed primarily as a store of wealth, such as a commodity backed coin (of which there had been attempts at such, like the old El Dorado (ELD)); then we generally can wait a few hours for confirmations without much harm done. At this point it becomes the difference between using debit cards vs. using bank wires, figuratively speaking of course. One can take weeks depending on banking laws, the other is instant.

The final major consideration we will look at in this chapter is the ease of use: For a cryptocurrency to be widely used and accepted, the installation and operation of its wallet must be easy enough so that everyone can do it without having to fiddle with settings and configurations, or have a massive amount of information technology knowledge and experience. It should work every time the software is launched and the wallet is opened, especially it needs to be functioning immediately after being installed the first time. I've found that only a small portion of cryptocurrencies have wallets that work seamlessly every time they are installed on a computer. Maybe one in ten work the way they are supposed to right "out of the box". Is this likely a Windows 10 problem? I almost believe it is. People do not seem to have the problems on Windows 7 or 8 like I am having on Windows 10 with various wallets working properly. To make matters worse, one wallet may work, but another wallet for another coin with the same technology will not. It is very irritating. It also instills a lack of confidence in prospective users and investors. If the wallet isn't going to work right, do they know what they are doing? If my coins are in a wallet and it stops working, do I lose everything? As long as you have your actual wallet file, your coins are going to be fine, but if you can never get the software working so that you can utilize those coins, that is a problem.

A non-user friendly wallet itself does not solely break a coin, but the less trouble the wallet is for using and storing a currency, the more people that likely will adopt it resulting in a much higher value per coin. Demand grows better when something is high quality, reliable, and user friendly.

The old Bikercoin wallet worked perfectly the first time every time, but the old Bitcoal (COAL) wallet, even though it uses the same core software as the old Bikercoin, did not install and work properly for everyone every time. Why? I do not know. Only people affected seem to be people like me running Windows 10.

Bitcoal was since taken up by new developers, and a brand new very smoothly operating PC based graphical user interface wallet was released. It is the nicest wallet I've seen for any currency, to be honest. Just shortly after this new wallet was released with the coin again having an active developer, a 340,000 COAL buy order went up on Cryptopia, at 112 SATs. Shortly after this happened, COAL rallied to 750 SATs before crashing to about 250 SATs. It has as of the end of Nov, 2017, been stable around 300 SATs, peaking to over 500 SATs now and then. This is how important an active developer, and a functioning high quality user friendly wallet makes to cryptocurrencies. *(www.getbitcoal.org for more info.)*

If a coin has been listed on a major exchange for a couple of years and hasn't gone away, it is probably a good coin, or at least one that will continue to be there especially if it has trade volume. The trade volume of any currency is essentially the "pulse" of a coin; the more trade volume in a day the stronger its vital signs. An added bonus is that exchanges such as Cryptopia give every coin a possible use; their exchange lets you list any item you wish to sell for any cryptocurrency that trades on their exchange, without any fees at all for utilizing their marketplace. Hopefully people become more accustomed to using their marketplace in the future, and if you can actually find something which will actually sell there for coinage, it will have the benefit of giving the currencies you are utilizing an actual boost to demand and therefore increase the real value of the coin.

People are very reluctant to part with their cryptocurrencies as they would rather hoard them up or day trade with them than buy things with it all. Yet, there are exceptions and all it takes is a few great exceptions to make your whole year a good one. The most impossible to find items generally end up being sold for cryptocurrencies, and usually things you can't buy anywhere but the internet are among these items.

Since the next step is to teach you about the entire opportunity itself followed by the mining or buying of cryptocurrencies depending on your strategy chosen, you might take some time now if you wish, to familiarize yourself with some of the various currencies and exchanges.

Coinmarketcap.com has the data on the majority of active currencies as well as the links associated with them and is probably your first place to browse around. Cryptopia.co.nz is another great place to start looking around and it is in my opinion the best exchange so I hereby give them my full endorsement, though I hope I can still give them my endorsement decades from now, but I can only speak for the here and now. They appear to be operating in compliance with their country's laws and regulations, and when they de-list currencies they give everyone time to withdraw all of their coins before shutting the currency down on their website.

I may not get around to revising this book in a timely manner if there is some bad news regarding my endorsements, so please verify that what few endorsements I have made are still valid before jumping in. I have always put my money where my mouth is, so, if I am wrong, it will cost me a lot. I am a member with other exchanges, but I only use Cryptopia because it is that much better of a user experience and I do not have to worry about the government seizing the servers with our coins on it. Cryptopia is one of the better designed exchanges with features as mentioned earlier that go far beyond the simple exchanging of one currency for another. Cryptopia specializes in Cryptonote/Forknote currencies, but I have not yet seen any coin that they have refused to add to the exchange if the listing fee is paid.

If you have seen a coin that you wish to know more about, or someone recommended a specific coin to you, then you can search for it on your favorite search engine, or follow the links provided on coinmarketcap.com for any coin you wish to know more about. There are forums, but I will not endorse any specific one. They are filled with drama, and very opinionated comments with very little of what is there capable of being taken at face value. Forums tend to be the primary realm of fear-mongers and disinformation, all rooted in bias one way or another. The primary value to be found in the forums is getting in on "day-one" of a new currency and keeping track of updates to the currencies which you are invested in already.

If you search the web for "cryptocurrency forum" you should have no problem finding the biggest ones in the business. I can't bring myself to advertise specific ones, for free, in my opinion they just haven't earned that level of respect from me, but since I need to give my readers a starting point, bitcointalk.org is perhaps the largest forum, and is one of the first places for new coins to be announced. The specifications of virtually every currency can be found in the coin's official threads in this forum, along with the important official links. Always keep an open mind when reading comments on those threads, criticism is usually unfounded, and praise can be self-serving. If someone succeeds in generating enough panic or enthusiasm with baseless claims, it will impact the market value, a coin could even crash for the perpetrator to buy up all the cheap coins ahead of the truth being found out.

Not all of the information provided to you regarding a given coin by search engine results will be honest or accurate, but it will at least give you some pros and cons for the given coins you are researching, in order that you may avoid the actual "cons"! Never believe advertisements for new coins at their face value; as Ronald Reagan said, "Trust, but verify."

There are also profitability calculators you will stumble upon which can help you decide what coins are more profitable to mine as well, since you want to maximize your return on mining investment. (*www.coinwarz.com is one such site offering more than just profitability calculations.*) Even if you are using your existing computer there is still the electricity cost to consider, though for most of us this is an "anyways" expense. You want to only mine the coins that you are certain offer you the best ROI either now or in the future. If you can get in on the first thirty days of mining on any cryptocurrency, you should do it! Coins are generally extremely easily mined in great abundance during the early days and it is a major key to successful portfolio building! A lot of miners wait a while because they automatically assume a new coin is the last thing the marketplace needs and that it therefore will be worthless, until it heads from SATs to KSATs and BTM's as they so often do. The majority of miners, mine for profit and if a coin is not yet listed on an exchange, they simply are not interested. Initial mining is generally done by speculators like me who want quantity before it gets listed, or by people who actually support and believe in the purpose and value of the coin.

No matter what coins you invest in, or what strategies you use to build your portfolio and fill your wallets with; always strive to avoid the bad coins. You don't have to necessarily buy into the best coins, but you need to find the undervalued best coins you can to reap the most benefit. It is hoped this chapter will help you avoid being wiped out from not asking the right questions before buying into just any currency.

Yes, things can and do change very fast in the cryptocurrency universe. I cannot calculate for these changes in what I am writing now, so if anything here becomes obsolete, view what I have said as a historical record and compare it to what has changed, thus you will have an example of just how dynamic this phenomenon is with the passage of even a short amount of time. It used to take centuries for empires to rise and fall; now the same happens within days, months, or even years in the world of cryptocurrency, all from the comfort of your own home. You have the power to be the armchair Napoleon of your own financial empire!

How many of you play *Railroad Tycoon*, or *Capitalism*, or any of the other business simulators? All you need to do is tell yourself this is a real life cryptocurrency tycoon game. You can leverage everything in those games with expert proficiency but you don't gain anything real; why not apply those skills of virtual empire building to real life endeavors and you shall prosper!

ADAM G. KOCH

PART IV: THE OPPORTUNITY ITSELF

Cryptocurrency is in the early stages of its existence *(it is a seven-year-old phenomenon as of this writing)* but look at every cryptocurrency that has become a monolith of success in a handful of years. Consider further that everything incredibly massive now was once incredibly small and struggling. Amazon started out in a basement; Microsoft started in a garage. The founders didn't start out with multinational multi-billion dollar enterprises. They *built* multi-national multi-billion dollar enterprises from scratch and taking risk. These founders had a dream, and dared to reach out and seize opportunity by the throat. Do you know why there is a "one-percent" in the first place?

For every one person who is self-made from understanding risk, reward and opportunity, there are ninety-nine more people who feel secure in their nine-to-five grind even though layoffs and downturns are inevitable which are most catastrophic when they do hit the job market. How do you keep a roof over your head and food on the table if your job no longer exists? We are conditioned to see security in things which are not secure like these jobs, careers and going to school to make sure we have degrees. It doesn't matter what you do for a living, you have no guarantees because even you aren't indispensable. If you build your own business, or make your own way in life you become indispensable so you cannot be fired or laid off. You see, working for yourself means in a good economy you will make more, in a bad economy you will make a bit less but you are still making it somehow.

The fact that as we draw nearer to the decade milestone since cryptocurrency entered the world stage and it is still booming with new all-time highs on a near daily basis means we are past the phase of having to worry about success or failure. It has succeeded, it will continue to succeed; but the cryptocurrency marketplace is going to be dynamic and highly volatile with its landslide movements up and down across the entire marketplace.

One of the facets of the opportunity before us, is that we can obtain massive quantities of less valuable currencies for a relatively small investment. It has long been said if you have a large enough quantity of anything it is worth a fortune. Look at all of the common things in the world; glass is practically worthless, yet companies make a fortune on glass because they can produce and distribute vast quantities of it cheaply enough to turn a profit, whereas you or I would never be able to pile up enough glass to make anything meaningful from it. *(Yes if we were really determined to make a living on glass, it could probably be done, but the logistics necessary would be such that if we could afford to get started would we really be poor enough to need to bother?)* You can buy bags of sand at the hardware store; you can even buy bags of manure for your gardens. People make money on the most common of things, but only by having mountains of the stuff and marketing it.

Economy of scale is what makes the kind of leverage we are interested in function to begin with. The more you have of something, the less the price needs to go up for you to make the kind of gains necessary for you to reach your goals of financial freedom. If you were able to buy one share of a stock for \$0.0001, and it goes up to \$0.01, that's a 10,000% ROI which is an outstanding profit, but in the end you are still worth only a penny on the deal. This is why you obtain cheap but useful and potentially valuable things in large, perhaps obscenely large quantities so that you can take advantage of economies of scale. Vast wealth comes from being able to obtain vast quantities of something for next to nothing that is reasonably certain to skyrocket in the near future. In fact, this is why insider trading is a big deal; if you know the future, you know which markets to corner. Just because something has a very low, perhaps almost free, price tag on it does not mean it is worthless. It just means the value and use has maybe not been perceived for what it actually is or will become.

Amongst the best indicators of the direction a currency price will swing is how large the buy orders are, and how small the sell orders are. Large sell orders close to the last trade value, indicate downward pressure if there is not much support in the buy orders; large buy orders indicate upward pressure on the price and will usually cause the sell orders to increase also in price if there is enough buying pressure.

Penny stocks are about as valuable as all the glass bottles you could ever hoard, until that fateful day when one piece of breaking news comes out and someone needs all your bottles so they are willing to pay a lot of money for them; or that one obscure company goes from $0.00001 a share to $0.01 or $1.00 a share. It may not have been overnight but it has happened with penny stocks but just not to everyone who's tried. The problem with penny stocks is you can always go broke and lose everything you ventured, but it is acceptable risk because you put up only a few dollars with the potential of making thousands or millions of dollars. Cryptocurrency shatters the traditional mold, and except in cases of total catastrophe you cannot be wiped out, and depending on your strategy, you won't have lost much anyways if the worst were to happen, but it is such a low failure rate when compared to penny stocks.

Whereas all coins are at some point exchangeable for Bitcoin and the cheapest all altcoins can ever be is one

Satoshi, or 0.00000001 of a BTC; this means the most worthless and most abundant, least liked, least used coin is going to be worth no less than $0.000080 at $8,000.00 per Bitcoin. It is very unusual for any altcoin to stay below ten SATs each for a long period of time if it is a relatively small quantity of coinage which exists. Primarily, a new coin starts out at the bottom, and then based on the hype and other aspects of its public image, the coin will either climb quickly or it will just smolder at a low price until it starts taking off after some time passes from people rallying to support the coin.

It is a common practice for those invested in a particular cryptocurrency to place buy and sell orders such that even though the price may not go very high, it does change often, the idea is to generate trade volume and make a small profit trading the spread between the buy and sell order prices. It is much quicker to trade some currencies than it is to mine them! Just as there are rolling stocks, there are rolling coins; that is cycles of high and low prices which repeat regularly and predictably over time, at least until it goes up and doesn't go back down where you want to buy.

The real value of altcoins can be found in their being much easier to mine than Bitcoin; as in you will receive more Bitcoinage indirectly as a result of mining altcoins with less electricity and hardware than you ever would mining Bitcoin directly. The Bitcoin mining difficulty is such right now that it costs thousands of dollars in hardware and electricity just to mine a few cents, perhaps a few dollars a year. If you want to invest a couple of thousand dollars into mining equipment, look at the various mining rigs available, run the numbers on the various profit calculators for the various coins, and you will see the altcoins are ranging from a few thousand dollars to as much as ten to twenty thousand dollars' profit in a year after electricity costs depending on the size of rig you buy and what coin you target. Someday though, the value of Bitcoin along with the amount of transaction fees in a block of

Bitcoins will make it closer to being worth mining even with smaller operations. One problem killing the Bitcoin mining for the small scale miners, is the fact that as the rewards drop and the prices go up, the big miners buy more mining hardware making it yet more difficult to mine the currency. All of this is adding to the perfect storm in forcing Bitcoin prices into the stratosphere.

In the event you decide to start mining cryptocurrency and don't know what to look for in terms of hardware, or how to build the best possible mining rig with your budget there is an upcoming part in this book where not only a lesson on mining, but also an overview of mining rigs will be presented. This will include a parts list to build the basic mining rig platform; you would just need to decide what graphics cards to add to it yourself. If you want to buy one that is already assembled and ready to go, advice for how to find the best value will be provided as well. There are crucial specifications which either will make a mining rig a bargain, or a costly blunder, which I also explain for your convenience.

As the mining difficulty increases, the price generally increases as well to offset the increased difficulty, and this holds true for most currencies. In other words, if there are many new miners working a particular coin all of a sudden, you will be able to expect a sharp rise in value. Miners will either shut down their rigs until it is profitable to run them again, or they will point them to mine other currencies which are compatible with their mining rigs. Not every coin can be mined on every rig. If you have a graphics card based rig, then you virtually can mine every currency there is, with some being greatly profitable and others being major losses; but mining a losing coin is still a winning proposition if you are merely trying to establish your holdings for speculation.

I have not seen any altcoin that has once been below five satoshis stay below five satoshis without being an actual scam coin. Currencies may spend much of their historical lifespan trading below there, but it will always be "pumped and dumped", which is what the practice of manipulating a coin's price to higher levels with the intention of dumping a massive amount of coins at a profit, in order to crash the price where they will rebuy the coins they sold at a bargain. As the prices increase, people get excited, add BTC to the market for trading, and this is usually the BTC the pumper/dumper takes as his profit. Those who are successful at this strategy are in fact able to corner a large percentage of a given crypto supply *and* increase their quantity of BTC at the same time. If a person wants to take a risk and is fast enough, it is possible to dump all of your coins before they do, and take your share of the profit they otherwise would have taken thus enriching yourself. It may not make sense now, but it will eventually. However, I have missed the dumps by thinking a rally was real and would be sustained; but have also missed real rallies by taking profits worried the crash was coming. So it is a mixed basket, and trading the spreads are the safest way to not lose your altcoin, or BTC but rather grow them reliably.

To demonstrate the ridiculous leverage we have when dealing with altcoins and to put it into perspective, let's look at a very mind-blowing example. Imagine seven years ago, when you could buy a Bitcoin for a nickel. Yes, I am talking very beginning when Bitcoin was just a novelty. If you bought a million Bitcoins, it would have cost say $50,000.00. Now... Are you ready for this? Those same coins would be worth $8 Billion dollars now. Never mind the fact that a mere thousand BTC is worth $8 Million dollars, an amount of money most of us will never earn in our entire lifetimes working our lives away. Just consider how cheap altcoins are right now, and look at how many did in fact go from nothing to many dollars each, and even hundreds of dollars.

If you look at real money, there was gold, silver, and copper. Copper has always has been considered the poor people's silver. Cryptocurrency tends to stratify the same way, that is into "gold", "silver" and "copper" type currencies.

You have the gold standard (Bitcoin), and then you have

altcoins which can be classified as either silver (Litecoin, Ethereum, Monero) or copper (Dogecoin and the vast majority of other altcoins including Bitcoal, and well, Coppercoin (COPPER)). Further consider that even copper, if you have enough of it, can make you rich. Butte, Montana after all, was built on primarily Copper. Cities were built in the past on Gold, Silver and other metals, but cryptocurrency will not build cities. It will however, build prosperity, and enable everyone regardless of their background or expertise to build their empire. It puts the power that was once monopolized by the elite bankers into the hands of we the people. Cryptocurrencies take everything you've ever wanted in life, and put all of these things within your grasp all due to the sheer amounts of leverage possible from them as an opportunity as a whole; the most ridiculously expensive things you could ever want in life even come within striking distance!

A good example of this leveraging principle can be explained thusly: What would you rather do if you had a thousand dollars to invest in the stock market? Would you buy five or ten shares of a big blue chip stock? Or would you find a cheaper stock that's either under a dollar or just a couple of dollars a share? If you manage to buy a thousand shares of a stock it is nice to think that for every dollar it goes up you've made a grand. But if you put it into ten shares of $100.00 a share stock, let's face it, it will go up a few dollars and then you've only made enough to buy dinner. It is unrealistic to expect a $100.00 a share stock to double or triple in price, but $1.00 a share stocks do it all of the time!

Cryptocurrencies work the same way. A hundred satoshis, or two hundred satoshis a coin is nothing, the coin is considered cheap and worthless still, yet if you can get them in bulk: These coins easily go into the thousands and ten thousand of satoshis on a regular basis if you know which ones and what their trading cycles are like. I had earlier this year bought 590 Prototanium (PR) at 4 KSATs each;

Prototanium went up to 18 KSATs weeks later and I sold them. In that same amount of time span, I am not aware of any stock in the market that has seen the same kind of ROI. There was only a supply of around a quarter million coins so I felt it was safe buying a low-supply coin that was also cheap. It may be stressful every time you pick a coin to speculate on that is new to you, but it is easier to be right more than you are wrong. If a coin drops after you buy into it, you can dollar-cost average it by buying more at the lower price reducing the average cost per coin, or you can just wait for it to head up again, it eventually will. Try not to buy on the peaks, but if you do, you only lose if you sell when it dumps. There will always be more pumping and dumping, because it is how so many people make money; so, wait until your coin you want rid of is at a price you are happy taking and sell if you are certain it will crash again.

The problem inherent with Bitcoin doubling, and it will double, but it will take a lot longer than is required for an altcoin to double; The market capitalization of Bitcoin at present, $170 Billion dollars. For Bitcoin to go to $20,000.00 per coin, the marketplace essentially has to expand by another $170 Billion Dollars. As more people dump more fiat money into Bitcoin, the more certain this doubling is to happen. On the other-hand, if Bitcoin goes from $10,000.00 to $5000.00, that is $85 Billion dollars in purchasing power lost across all Bitcoins held by everyone collectively. That is a lot of money that can go into thin air, but, it came out of thin-air also! So, let's say the market cap of Bitcoin is still well over 130 million ounces of gold; while you would lose the equivalent value of 65 million ounces of gold if Bitcoin halved right now, this is what sets cryptocurrency apart from precious metals. You can't make 65 million ounces of gold disappear into thin air (without the art of illusion of course).

Just to clarify, the market capitalization does not mean that is how much money is there at all times actually backing up the Bitcoins; It just means at the present market value, that is the fair market value of all of the Bitcoins mined so far. It is the price at which the last person selling and the last person buying struck a bargain on. If you have a very large quantity of Bitcoins to sell, you could maybe crash the market value by thousands of dollars. Chances are though, there is enough money actually there to absorb a huge sale without significantly reducing the price.

All cryptocurrencies have no real price until they are used or sold, then whatever you bought with them or whatever you were paid for them is what they were actually worth.

If a company has a million shares that are a dollar a share, that's a million dollars in market cap, but if it goes to $0.50 a share, where did the half a million dollars in wealth go? You can have millions of dollars in stock market wealth, but when it crashes, all of that money is gone and no one has any of it, because stocks, like cryptocurrencies, are backed up by what people will pay in the future for them and not what has already been paid for them or into them. It is just the people who sold off first before a crash are better off than those who waited for it to hit the bottom. Even then you aren't really taking a loss at all until you sell low. Once you sell low, you have actually taken your loss, just as once you sell high you've taken your gains. With the caveat that if the price keeps climbing up after you've sold at what you thought was the high price, that future increase in price represents your opportunity cost for having sold out too soon.

By now, you've heard a lot of these things a few times, and yes, this is the chapter where we get down to the specifics about the opportunity. In fact, this whole book should have given you the understanding behind this opportunity, but we need to look at *how* you can participate in the opportunity. How do you get started and make it work for you?

The first way to participate is to mine your cryptocurrency, which is largely free you only need electricity (which you use anyways when you are gaming and etc. except when you aren't gaming you can be making cryptocurrency with your computer) and a computer with internet access, preferably broadband though the bandwidth utilization is almost nothing for mining activities. This is usually how we all started out. It gives you practical hands-on experience which will carry you on into your future ventures. As a result of having cryptocurrency, you will begin to learn how to exchange your first coins, and what uses they will serve for you.

If you want to expand your mining operations, building or buying mining rigs is not so difficult if you can afford to do so, considering they can pay themselves off within a few months thereby leaving the rest of their useful lifetime to earn you profit even though these rigs can run into the thousands of dollars depending on what you mine and how much processing power you want. The graphics cards are the most expensive part of a mining rig. There are some mining operations that are so massive people do not have to heat their houses in the winter from the mining rigs producing heat as a byproduct of all the computing and energy usage. Don't let this discourage you, it takes a rather massive operation to heat your whole house. In the summer time, this is not a problem if you have a safe place to run it perhaps in a garage or in your basement where the heat would be absorbed by a naturally cool environment. In the worst case, you will want to run some air-conditioning in the summer with a mining operation.

The second option, is to invest an amount of money as you are able on a regular basis. Mining may not appeal to you, and maybe you want to start seeing instant results. There are people who have done very well by setting aside a percentage of their income every payday into Bitcoins. It is safe to do right now, Billionaires are diversifying into cryptocurrency now, bankers are buying it up, governments are said to be setting up Bitcoin mining operations also. In other words, the very experts at making markets move, are getting involved. They are not getting involved to lose money, they are getting involved because it represents the future. Wealthy people, and banks all are large holders of gold and silver. Why? Every paper money that has ever existed in the history of the world up until our current money system; all fiat money systems crashed terribly, and gold and silver always sprung up in the wake of these crashes. Mankind has always returned to sound money; the wealthy people know this, and they know they are stockpiling real money when they buy gold and silver with paper. They are ready for fiat to crash and go away.

(Bitcoins are easier and cheaper to buy than mine unless you obtain them through mining altcoins; there aren't a lot of options for U.S. buyers to purchase BTC due to anti money laundering laws and the Patriot Act. many exchanges do not want to bother complying with the regulations so do not accept U.S. customers. Virtual World Exchange, or Virwox.com lets you buy BTC for PayPal, but they have layered fees. You have to convert USD into Second Life Lindens, where they get a heavy commission (like 15%), and then from Second Life Lindens, into BTC (around another 15%). If it is your only option, it is a bargain despite the highway robbery. Coinbase, and other exchanges sell BTC for fiat, but I do not know if they have changed their policy towards U.S. buyers purchasing with USD. The forums may actually have information for more friendly buying and selling of BTC for U.S. users.)

If you put aside a couple percent of your income or even ten percent of it, your portfolio will grow nicely over time, especially when you take advantage of altcoins and their leverage potential for turning your BTC into more BTC *(and more altcoins too).*

There is always something coming along, requiring every last cent I have had just to get through it. Had I actually forced myself to put five or ten percent of my income for the last few years into Bitcoin and altcoins without drawing it all down, I would be worth millions right now, literally and I am not joking. I knew I needed to do it, but I just couldn't seem to make it happen. That is the human element that tends towards failure along with life happening as it does. I've learned my lesson, and now I am playing catch-up while there is still time.

Times are still tough for a lot of people and coming up with five or ten percent to sock away is a challenge. Your vehicle to get to work always breaks down and needs repairs, or your washer and dryer break down. I was planning to have this book done six months ago, but in six months I had to rewrite most of this book because the price of Bitcoin went up so much, and I actually learned a lot about a lot more things which I am presenting to you in this book.

I would have given you this same advice to set some of your income aside for BTC back then also; Bitcoin has gone from $1250 and $2,000 then, to $12,000 and it backed off back to $10,000 where it holds steady now. It takes hundreds, even thousands of hours to actually produce a book of quality ready for publication which meets everything it was written for. I tried to rush production of this project, but it is only now I could actually bring it into the completion phase. In all of this time you could been gaining had you known to put some aside into BTC then, but it is what it is. There is a lot of growth left in Bitcoin, so all we can do is make sure we don't miss out on it again.

You know about this opportunity now, and believe me, it is worth cutting a few bucks off of your spends if you have to in order to avail yourself to invest something in it, that is if you decide not to start out mining altcoins with your computer. I would rather make my own coffee at home and save the $3.00-$5.00 a day on coffee to invest in my future freedom than to make some big corporation wealthy on the markup when all I get for buying their coffee is an empty cup! I remember when Bitcoins were $5.00 each. People would go and buy expensive espressos and some were buying two or three a day! That was between one and three BTC they were throwing away in opportunity cost each day! So ultimately in finding just the right amount of tradeoff between building your empire with no investment, and actually investing something; it is up to you to decide what your financial freedom is worth to you. Everyone who built something truly great had sacrificed greatly to achieve it. They weren't just sacrificing luxuries, but necessities too. Fortunately, now, the average person has enough luxuries that can be sacrificed for a while if that's the route you decide to go.

If you will mine your altcoins to start out with, trading your mined coins can grow your cryptocurrency balances in no time, but it requires a certain nerve to do so. Every time you take a profit by selling an altcoin, you are praying you don't have to watch it go up to a point that would have made you wealthy had you held on to it. If on the other hand you are able to buy and sell a coin repeatedly in short amounts of time, it will indeed grow your holdings very quickly; which is what we attempt to do when we "trade the spread".

Whether you mine or just put a portion of your income into cryptocurrencies, some trading will be necessary, but trading isn't something everyone feels comfortable doing on a regular basis. I have friends who trade regularly making a quarter of a Bitcoin here and a quarter of a Bitcoin there from taking profits and then reinvesting them into other coins or waiting for the price to drop on the coins they just sold to buy them back in a greater quantity at a lower price. Some coins at any given time are ripe for using this method.

The best part of this type of trading with cryptocurrencies is you can day trade all you want, as mentioned before, the stock market requires investors in the United States to have a minimum amount of portfolio value to be eligible to day-trade. At the time when I was actively trading stocks, it was $25,000.00 that an investor was required by Regulation T to have. You were allowed to have a round-trip, that is a buy and a sell, once in three days.

Regulations are the war machine of choice with which the elite wage their class warfare on the "lower strata." These are regulations invented strictly to keep the lower strata from growing their own empires and breaking their bonds of debt with all of the usury attached to it. There are a lot of young people smart enough to make their fortunes at a young age if only they were allowed to take what wealth they have and be allowed to leverage it with every bit of their know-how; but to have to save up $25,000.00 to be able to day-trade? That is a lot of sweat equity to pile up and a lot of sacrifice to go without in order to reach that goal, all while hoping you avoid all major catastrophes in life which could dry it all up on you. Even with the one round-trip every three days' rule, I still was able to leverage $1200.00 into nearly $4,000.00 in a single month on the stock market. Then, I did the unthinkable. I bought some penny stocks, and did not sell when they went up, and then the bottom fell out completely washing me up. If you ignore your wealth, it will go away, believe me. Think about it though... $25,000.00 for the average wage slave, is a couple year's income before you are allowed actual day-trading privileges.

Why bother trading cryptocurrencies? Well, I can think of no better reason right now than every BTM you gain, is $9-$12. You do not have to make too many nine or twelve dollar bills before your net-worth climbs to a respectable level! Besides, you can gain an awful lot of altcoins that when they finally do head into the several dollars per coin range themselves, will make you very wealthy.

The last way to obtain coinage, of course is to buy and sell real things for cryptocurrency. If you offer something valuable, even on craigslist if you had to, and say you are willing to accept cryptocurrency, you can be sure offers will come in. There are people now selling cars and trucks on craigslist saying they will accept Bitcoin! That is a far cry from just a few years ago when the very mention of the word sent people running for the hills or screaming in fright.

There have been instances where someone learns you are into Bitcoin and before you can tell them anything about it out come those words... "Oh my God! You've joined a cult!" I am not kidding. Or they will say, "What did you do that for? Now you are a criminal! Criminals use them! No honest person would have anything to do with them!" Of course that is further from the truth than any lie or disinformation could ever be. BTC is probably used in relation to very little crime right now due to the fact authorities have learned how to track the transactions and link them to the individuals who used them for criminal purposes. The criminal element has jumped ship by and large, heading for other currencies like Monero. People genuinely were scared of Bitcoin, once upon a time. They didn't understand it, and when you don't understand something you generally hate it. In a few years of BTC going mainstream and setting new records almost daily, the general attitude amongst the population is changing in favor of it.

The more mainstream it goes, the more people who are involved, the more upward pressure there will be. There is no better time than now to get in on this opportunity, which to summarize is something like this: Bitcoin buys altcoins, altcoins trade and grow so when sold, you have even more Bitcoin than you bought in the first place. Or, mining altcoins, gives you a net worth of BTC that you can just watch grow as your portfolio grows.

If you need one more way to grow your portfolio, referral programs exist for some of the exchanges whereby you earn a small percentage of the fees collected on trades they have made for having signed up under you. If you are an excellent affiliate marketer or great at social networking, then it could very much be a real opportunity to take part in as a way to generate cryptocurrency without any overhead.

I almost forgot, there are "faucets", which serve the purpose of trickling a cryptocurrency into circulation by awarding random preset amounts to visitors to the faucet who follow the instructions provided. Not all currencies will have faucets, but many do. Cryptopia does in fact have a chat window, and sometimes people will give away their altcoins as a way of promoting a currency they wish to see succeed through a feature called "tipping." I've never yet received any tips, but then I haven't been using the chat window much at all; except I have given some coinage out before so I know it works. Fair warning though, exchange chatrooms are not always what I would call family friendly, so you kind of need to have a tough hide if you dare participate in them, and there is no shortage of obscene material circulating around on them so keep small eyes away. Most of the time they are hidden by default until you click the tab for it to pop out of the side of the browser window meaning you won't be subjected to things you might not want to see.

There is no right way to build your strategy, though there are wrong ways. Obviously you do not wish to buy high and sell low. Dollar-cost averaging will allow you to reduce average cost of each coin, should you buy some only to have the price drop. Do not be afraid to examine the charts and trading history, there are many clues to be found in these resources. Always check the distribution of buy and sell orders. The stronger they are closer to the last price, the more stable the coin is. Don't get greedy, don't get anxious, and never panic. I have lost more because of panic than I have by not panicking and waiting things out.

Now that you've been given the "tour" as it were, it's time to get down to the business end of things. This very next part of the book is going to give you a detailed look at exchanges and how they work, even how to use them.

PART V: CRYPTO TRADING & EXCHANGE

It would not be right of me to teach you all about this wonderful opportunity, only to leave you distressed over not knowing how to actually utilize the key components upon which the entire opportunity depends. If you don't know how to use the exchanges, or if you do not know how to utilize the information available on them, that is what this section is here for! It might not be an *advanced* trading course, but you definitely will be able to begin your journey!

This part's whole purpose is to take a single exchange, and break most of it down for you, step by step, and yes, I will do my best to add graphics to aid you in seeing what I am talking about. The actual fundamentals that will impact your decision to buy, sell, or hold the cryptocurrencies you possess will be generally explained in some depth. Some of you will be able to figure it out if you skip this section; but remember, if you skip it, you can always come back to it should you grow confused.

Since virtually all exchanges work the same way, they will have roughly similar features. Some exchanges go very far with what they offer you in terms of analytics and tools, others are basic and poorly designed almost to the point of irritation. I am choosing to use Cryptopia.co.nz as my teaching aid so that you can learn your way around exchanges and I will show you the various tools at your disposal and how to spot a relatively safe buy, and relatively unsafe buys utilizing these tools. Actually, I don't know if you can call them tools, they just added more functionality than most exchanges seem to which we can use to our advantage.

I am only affiliated with Cryptopia to the extent that I have a referral link and it only benefits me if you are kind enough to type it in as mentioned earlier in the book; Cryptopia did not pay me to feature them here, nor do I owe them any favors, except only from recognizing them as a truly amazing exchange doing a spectacular service for their users. In my opinion, not only as a cryptocurrency miner and trader, but as a user of cryptocurrency, I am firmly convinced that it is the best and most well-rounded exchange out there. It is the only one I have found thus far offering a marketplace in which any listed currency on the exchange is usable for the payment of purchases if agreed to between the buyer and seller, all while taking no buyers or sellers fees when a deal is struck.

In the future year and decades to come, I may have to pull my endorsements should a project or exchange be ruined by new owners or developers, or if anything major goes wrong with them. I do not anticipate having to pull any endorsements as I have that much faith put into them, but times change now and then. Many things in this book are subject to change; prices, links, endorsements too. Always read everything within the context and timeframe it was written and then compare what "was" now as I write, to what is "now" when you are reading this. If there are *major* changes to be addressed, yes, I will publish a new edition and Amazon will notify all Kindle customers of the update once they agree the changes are significant enough to warrant replacing your old edition with the new one, in which case the second digital edition will be free if you already bought this first edition. If I do have to publish a new edition, then of course I will update everything that is out of date, and add anything meaningful which may further benefit my readers, past and present.

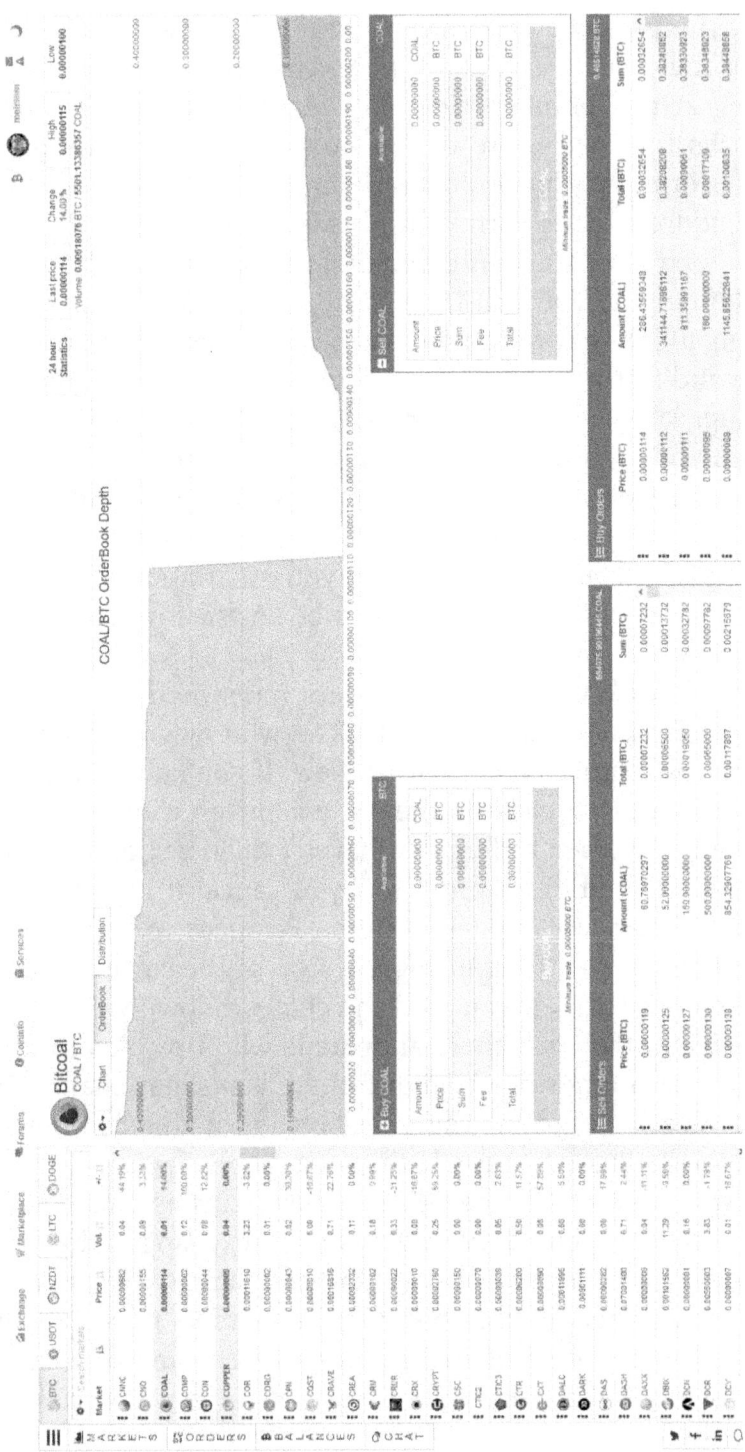

So, the previous page has as large of a view as I can give you of the exchange. It is not necessary to be able to read the writing at this point in time, but feel free to turn the book sideways to make sense of the image! The registration is a simple form, in which you simply put your name, username, email address along with your password. It is so simple that I really don't need to go into detail of the registration form, so I am skipping it. You will then have to confirm your email by clicking a link they send you, and yes I will explain how to set up second factor authentication which will keep you safe from hacking, later on in this portion of the book. I will further explain how you create a wallet and add or remove cryptocurrency from this exchange as well. For right now, since you do not have any coins if you have only just created a Cryptopia account, I will give you a run-down on the essentials you will need to know to be an effective coin trader and find your way around.

-*Left Panel:* Very left column lets you switch between the Market, Orders, Balances, and Chat windows. The current view in the picture is the Market view. If you have placed any buy or sell orders, clicking the Orders button will show you a list of all your open orders that haven't filled yet, and clicking the X at the end of an order lets you cancel it if you need a quick and easy way to get to them. Balances will show your wallet balances, without losing the view of the current market you are on. Chat, lets you load the chat window, which if you are active in the chat, there are people who tip coins to users as a way of promoting them and there is a slight chance you might receive some. At the very bottom of this column are social media link buttons which no one probably uses.

-*List Column*: In the Market view, this is the column which lists every currency trading on the exchange. Above the search box, are alternative coin markets, that is, you can trade altcoins for other altcoins, but not every altcoin turns into any altcoin, only specific ones. You may search for the name or ticker symbol of a coin to find it easier, or you may just use the alphabetical list, or sort it any way you wish. From high to low, from Z to A, whatever is most useful to you. Coins you own seem to turn blue in the list. On the left portion of this column, you have Ticker Symbols; COAL is Bitcoal, COPPER is Copper Coin, LTC is Litecoin, etc. Every ticker is unique, no two coins are allowed to have the same ticker at the same time or it will cause a conflict when the two coins try to appear on the same exchange, and also it may cause issues when trying to be listed on coinmarketcap.com which is very essential to success of any coin. If in the Bitcoin marketplace, you will see the Price is denoted in decimal forms of Bitcoin, the right most digit after the decimal is the single Satoshi digit. As you go left, it works just like regular numbers. Tens, Hundreds, Thousands, Ten Thousand, then it goes to BTMs, and the first digit to the left of the decimal is of course whole entire Bitcoins. The Vol. column just tells how much activity there is in terms of Bitcoin down to the hundredths of a BTC. When you click on a coin it will tell you down to the satoshi in the upper right, along with the quantity of the coin traded to make that BTC volume. Then, last on this column, is the +/- which indicates the increase or loss for the past twenty-four hours. Just these numbers alone do not tell the whole story, however.

-Very Top Horizontal Bar: Left to right, you have home button for Cryptopia home page, then the exchange button brings you to the market view of the exchange. Marketplace takes you to the part of the site where people list and sell things for cryptocurrency. You can list things for sale from this page. Forums, takes you to the forums of course. The next two options, Coininfo and Services are miscellaneous features I haven't needed to use yet and you may not need to worry about them either. To the very right of this bar, is a Bitcoin symbol, if you mouse over it, you have the option to go to Balances, Deposit, Withdraw, Transfer. To the right of that, where your username appears, gives you the option to go to your user account information, change settings such as set

up two factor authentication, change passwords and etc.; and of course the support tab. After that, you have the notification indicator, such as when your orders fill, or if you get messages. If you have items listed in the marketplace, you will receive an email notifying you and it will also tell you here in this list also. The next button, lets you switch from the view you see, a white background and colored text and charts; to a night time view that is easier on the eyes in a dark room, with a dark grey/black background with grey buttons and appropriate light text that works rather well. I prefer the night time mode, but it would not show well because the paperback of this book prints the inside pictures in grayscale, so I am showing the day-time default mode.

Charts- Above the charts on the left, you have a Coin looking symbol. This is the digital coin's "official" appearance, merely an avatar, but it makes them distinctive especially when popularity soars and it becomes fashionable to have merchandise made out of these logos, not to mention physical coins will be made in this image if ever they are made. The name of the currency is to the right of the logo, and below it is the Ticker / Market Currency. In this case it is COAL / BTC as it is showing the BTC market for COAL.

The actual chart itself, there are three charts, pictured is the Order Book Depth. This I only recently learned of and I am rather sad I didn't learn about it sooner; it is a very powerful tool for evaluating a currency. You see, it represents the supply and demand for a current coin at present time.

The left side, is how many coins' people want to buy for various prices. The further to the left, the lower the price those coins are ordered at. The line rises as it goes to the left, because it is telling you how much Bitcoinage is essentially backing the coin. At any point if you mouse over a price-point, it tells you how many BTM's you will get right now if you sell that many of the coins. It starts with the first order which is highest on the buy order list, and then as you go down, all of those lower orders are cumulative and is what the graph is built out of. On the right side, you have all of the coins available if you want to buy them 'now' and not wait for someone else to sell to your buy order.

The biggest problem with altcoins has been, they can be very hard to obtain a lot of, then after you finally do and you want to sell, how much liquidity do they have? COAL, at this moment in time, is very liquid. In order for the price to crash, those orders must be cancelled, or someone actually has to dump that many coins. Imagine this as a load-bearing structure; the left is the supporting column and the thicker it is towards the current market price, the more support there is for it at the present price point. If the right side of the chart is much larger than the left, those people waiting to sell their coins might grow impatient and take what they can get, causing that column to collapse. I tend to think of the right side as how much "weight" the left side, the support column, has to actually support. In this instance, it is not worth a market manipulator's time to dump all or most of their currency to barely impact the lower price point with the purpose of putting in an even lower buy order.

If all of the COAL sell orders were pulled and dumped, it would barely put a dent in the market price. And notice how thin that graph starts out on the right, it has to go up quite high in price before there are any quantities of COAL to buy. If you actually want COAL now, you will have to pay a premium to get them, forcing the market up. So, all in all, this is a strong indicator that COAL is a sound investment. Combine this with all the other fundamentals, this really is a solid buy right now. It is poised to climb, who knows how high. It will likely double soon at least. It may take time for investors and users to find out how good of a buy it actually is, but it has little indication of risk for me to worry about it crashing. *(COAL hit 750+ SATs w/ 20 BTC volume the day after I wrote this.)*

You will notice there is a gap between the buy and sell orders. This is the spread I was telling you about! This is where you can harvest your trading profits in a stable market. At this particular point in time when the image was made, the lowest "sell" order (which means coins available for purchase right now that others are selling) is 119 Satoshis. The highest "buy" order, meaning if you wanted to sell coins you have, is 114 Satoshis. This makes a spread of five Satoshis. If you place coins for sale at 119 Satoshis, or even 118 Satoshis, if they sell before the spread changes, you can place a buy order for 113 Satoshis here.

(There are so many coins wanting to be bought in this example at 112 Satoshis, with orders being filled in the order they were placed, you may never get your replacements bought. If there is plenty of spread, you can beat the highest order to get your coins back. If something happens and you are not able to rebuy before the entire market climbs higher, you might be out of luck, like everyone who sold Bitcoin at $250.00 but had to rebuy at $750.00 because they feared Bitcoin would keep going higher leaving them behind. Choose a portion of your coins that you don't mind risking but are happy with the gains on successful trades. Always keep a significant amount of a good coin for when it does significant increase. If the highest buy order has a low quantity, you are safe to match the price of your own buy order.)

Coin Balance Distribution View

The distribution tab below the logo on the previous page, shows a bar chart of Cryptopia users' coin balance distribution. The horizontal lines in this example each represent 100,000 COAL. As you can see, the number one holder of coins in the exchange, possesses just short of half a million COAL (495,049 and some change) which is quite impressive. If you mouse over on each bar, it shows you the exact balance, but it is usually enough to see side-by-side comparisons.

You will be able to judge if most of the coins are in the hands of a few, or if they are fairly evenly distributed, or confirm there are actually more than just a few people using a given coin! Yes, these balances include those coins still waiting for sell orders to execute. Over time, you can watch how the coin's distribution changes, i.e. if more big investors come in. This does not count the coins these people may have withdrawn into their PC wallets; only what they have on the exchange right now to put towards selling. While there are enough coins on the exchange to dump the coal price a little way, it is not in their best interest to do so right now. As the price goes up, if the support becomes thinner and thinner, and there is a lot more weight as it climbs, it just might be the indicator to take profits before these big holders do. All of the information the exchange provides can be read into and used somehow. The smaller the largest holdings become, generally the more favorable the market price will be to increasing. Anonymity is still preserved, you can't see who is holding these.

Default Chart View

The default chart view, is the chart that you will see first upon clicking on a coin in the exchange. It is the kind of chart most of us are familiar with from watching the stock market or who knows, maybe we even paid attention in school during math classes. It is the living monument to the old "buy high sell low" philosophy we have all heard, and it also demonstrates hindsight is twenty-twenty.

It is very customizable allowing you to view the time period you want to see, and how closely you want to look at it. Again, I apologize the pictures are what they are, but feel free to open the website and explore it. I only wanted to show the aerial view of the concepts anyways, which even at this scale these images should convey.

The height of each stick displayed in the chart, represents the two prices between which the coin had traded for on that particular time unit. If you mouse over each stick of the chart, you will see the numbers above them in the upper right corner changing. This number will tell you the volume traded, how much BTC worth of trades, and other important information such as the exact high and the exact low for that day. The long solid line below without bars, reflects the trade volume, so you can compare the trade volume to the price changes with ease. You may further alter the details of the chart such as changing the trading period reflected by the sticks, and how far back in time or how recent the whole thing presents data for. Really, it doesn't need a lot of explanation as it is all pretty standard.

-Buying Coins

Assuming you've deposited some BTC or sold some mined coins for BTC and have a balance to buy and you want to buy some coins, here is how you do it. In this example (you can choose your own coins of course, this is just an example), there are 3,853 COAL for sale at 0.00000122 BTC each. Total investment required to buy them now, would be 4.7 BTM's rounded up, or .00470068 to be exact. Click on that order, and it will pre-populate the fields in the Buy COAL window, as shown in the following image. If you only wanted to buy say, a thousand COAL, you would click in the "amount" field, and change it to "1000" and generally you do not need to use commas, on some exchanges trying to use them may cause errors executing your trade.

Changing the amount of COAL, will change the Sum, and the Fee line to reflect the new amount of COAL that you are buying. Review the numbers and verify the accuracy, and push the Buy COAL button when ready; if in the time you were setting up your purchase there was not enough COAL left at the price specified, a buy order will be placed at 122 Satoshis for the difference that was not available, and it will eventually fill if someone wants to sell to you at that price.

If you needed 4,500 COAL, just click far enough down for there to be a large enough quantity, then revise the amount to 4,500 and it will automatically buy up to that as cheaply as possible paying appropriately as the price climbs if you did not want to wait for a "buy" order to fill at a lower price. (Too large of buy orders can make prices go up.)

Buy COAL		Available: 0.00000000 BTC
Amount	3853.01877159	COAL
Price	0.00000122	BTC
Sum	0.00470068	BTC
Fee	0.00000940	BTC
Total	0.00471009	BTC

Buy COAL

Minimum trade: 0.00005000 BTC

Sell Orders			666845.61916090 COAL
Price (BTC)	Amount (COAL)	Total (BTC)	Sum (BTC)
0.00000122	3853.01877159	0.00470068	0.00470068
0.00000123	43.24499651	0.00005319	0.00475387
0.00000125	52.00000000	0.00006500	0.00481887
0.00000127	150.00000000	0.00019050	0.00500937
0.00000130	500.00000000	0.00065000	0.00565937

The orders can be as large as you need, or as small as you want as long as the minimum BTC value is met; recently it has become a .00005 BTC minimum, or 5 KSATs worth of coinage, which is ok, it is a small minimum, and the trading fees are very reasonable at a mere fraction. You may also place many different orders at many different amounts if and when you deem it beneficial to do so, and you can always cancel these orders if they do not fill in which case you lose nothing.

-Selling Coins

Naturally, this works sort of the same way as buying, but backwards. In this example, I clicked the highest Sell order which was 122 Satoshis, but since I wanted to undercut them, I changed it to 121 Satoshis as pictured below. I only wanted to sell 1,000 COAL, which would net me .00120758 of a BTC. If the order sells successfully, I can turn around and place a buy order for 1,057 COAL at 114 Satoshis, which is an increase of fifty-seven COAL when this buy order fills. It depends on how much trade activity there is on a coin; however, even if it takes a whole day for this order to fill, that means I earned 57 COAL in one day! (Selling too many at once can drop prices.)

☐ Sell COAL		Available: 161881.78940184 COAL
Amount	1000	COAL
Price	0.00000121	BTC
Sum	0.00121000	BTC
Fee	0.00000242	BTC
Total	0.00120758	BTC

Sell COAL

Minimum trade: 0.00005000 BTC

☰ Buy Orders			0.49260944 BTC
Price (BTC)	Amount (COAL)	Total (BTC)	Sum (BTC)
0.00000113	11361.52987308	0.01283853	0.01283853
0.00000112	341144.71698112	0.38208208	0.39492061
0.00000111	811.35991167	0.00090061	0.39582122
0.00000100	14949.17281244	0.01494917	0.41077039
0.00000095	180.00000000	0.00017100	0.41094139

Yes, fifty-seven COAL does not sound like much, 6kSAT isn't a big fortune. However, it is the mechanism by which that COAL is earned that is significant. If you can find a very active coin with a good spread, imagine if you could have done that to 100,000 coins. Then, you would have 5,700 extra coins, with a value of about 6BTM instead! That is nearly $50.00 right now, which on a busy coin, would be a few minutes maybe a few hours' work. On less active coin like COAL, well, it might take a day or more but inevitably the orders do fill. There are coins with a lot more spread, which are very lucrative if you get in on them at the right time. Start with small amounts until you get a handle on doing it. Mistakes are less painful when small, and profits much more grand when you have mastered the art of trading.

What's further is, the average coin, even if almost worthless, is still not going to be very easily mined unless you were in on those first tens of thousands of blocks. There are fairly new currencies that I can barely mine any coins on as there is so much mining power directed at them. So, if I make this 57 COAL on this one trade, who knows, it might be more than I would have made trying to only mine them. You can also trade at the same time you are mining, too. Nothing says you can't do both! *(Based on current difficulties, and my laptop's hashing power, the calculator for COAL says I can currently mine an estimated 48 coins a day. So, in one single small trade, I made more than I can mine in a day!)* DO NOT confuse the buy box with the sell box! It CAN wipe you out.

-Depositing Coins to the Exchange

One of the ways to obtain coins with which to trade, is through mining, or selling items. However, you come into possession of your coins, you may want to put them into the exchange, or remove some from the exchange. This is accomplished in the Balance menu.

You will see there is an option to hide zero balances (makes it easier to find the coins you actually own) but if you are looking to deposit a currency you do not yet have, make sure this box is unchecked. You may type in the name, or the ticker symbol into the search box and it will show you the matching currency. Clicking on the button showing the green arrow pointing into a rectangle, which is the very left button unless they change it some day; is the deposit button. When you click that, it will give you a prompt saying "generating address." It will then show you all the relevant information you need for depositing that type of currency from other sources. Specifically, you will need to open your online or PC wallet and find your send button, paste the address for your Cryptopia wallet for that coin into the address field in your send window, along with the quantity of coinage you wish to deposit to the exchange.

Always double check the accuracy of all forms before you hit send, mistakes can result in lost funds, and always look for fine print or any notations which are there to warn you about certain precautions to take. For instance, Cryptopia warns not to use your exchange wallets to receive mining pool payouts. If mining, you will want a PC wallet working, or an online wallet if there is one available for your currency, that your mining payouts can be sent to. Once you have the coins in your wallet you can deposit them yourself by sending to the address specified in your exchange wallet for that currency.

-Withdrawing

Withdrawing works similarly, except in the exchange, you click the withdraw button, which is the button with the red arrow pointing away from the rectangle. It will then ask for the address to send the currency to, and the quantity of currency to withdraw. You may be sent an email requiring you to click the link to confirm the withdrawal. Enter your Two Factor code if applicable. When copying and pasting wallet addresses, be sure there are no extra characters.

-Transfers

There is another button. Two arrows pointing opposite directions, which represents the Transfer button. If you owe someone cryptocurrency such as buying items in the

Cryptopia marketplace, or if you were to buy or sell cryptocurrency in person, or any number of other possibilities: Instead of using a withdraw, click on this transfer button on the same row as the currency to be transferred is listed, and then put the recipient's username into the appropriate field. Before it lets you send the currency, it will confirm the user exists and you also can see if it is the right recipient. Very simple. No fees are charged for these transfers. If you need to pay someone who does not have a Cryptopia account, then you will need to use the Withdraw button instead.

-*Miscellaneous*

If you click on your account name to bring up the whole menu. Everything you need to do for securing and keeping your account up to date or changing options, can be found here.

-Account – Profile Details: You have the option of making this information public, but by default it is private. The information is optional; you are not required to provide it. On the right of this page you will find your referral link, and a report on how many referrals you have along with your share of the trade fees collected. Whenever possible, it is wise to share your referral links with anyone you tell about the site.

-Settings: Not much to see here, but if you want to disable annoying notifications this is where to do it, and also to ignore chat users.

-Security: This is where you can set up your two-factor authentication method. I do not recommend any two-factor authentication that requires the Google authenticator app; my phone broke and it took days to regain access to all of my accounts as the authenticator app did not port over to the new phone with all of my credentials when I installed it on the new phone. The first time I had this problem, it worked fine, the second time, it didn't work. So, I no longer trust Google for this. I recommend a PIN code or any method that works best for you.

Two-factor authentication is very important. There are massive lists sold on the black market that contain email addresses, usernames and passwords; a lot of people reuse passwords. This makes a certain percentage of accounts automatically vulnerable to brute-force attacks. With two-factor authentication, they can have a successful login with your information, but they won't be allowed into your account without correctly responding to the second factor challenge.

-Messages: This is the exchange messaging system. You can contact other users directly through this part of the site, and read messages that have come in.

-Notifications: This is where you can see what has been happening; as orders fill or things sell, you will receive notifications. Also if you receive messages or something.

-Balances: We already covered this in depth earlier.

-Open Trades: Already covered earlier.

-Market Items: This is where you see all of the items you have listed on the Cryptopia market place. It is essential for managing your listed items.

-Karma: When you do something good, like give away coinage in the chat, people will reward you with Karma. It simply tells people you have interacted positively with the community to some extent.

-Term Deposits: Discontinued in order to comply with trading regulations, so yes, Cryptopia is above-board.

-Paytopia Payments: I have no clue. Have not used or needed this page in my couple years of using Cryptopia.

-History: The various kinds of history for your accounts activities will be found at the bottom of this menu.

Now that you have had a crash course in exchanges and using them, it is time to look at obtaining coinage. If you wish to mine your currency, that is what the very next part of the book is dedicated to.

If you want to buy your cryptocurrency, it all starts with Bitcoin. Some people find sites that let you buy Bitcoin from local people whom you meet up with to pay them and transfer the coinage. This allows smaller fees, but I find it a hassle to deal with other people, I just can't be bothered with it. eBay is an option, but high fees are involved, and it is uncertain if people are selling coins they actually have ready to pay you, or if they are actually mining contracts since eBay changed how cryptocurrencies are listed. They want ready-to-sell coinage listed as expensive classified ads. Mining contracts can still be listed as standard eBay listings. A mining contract is only an agreement to mine you a specified amount of currency, or sell you the future production of their mining rigs for a specified period of time.

I would avoid cloud-mining websites; a friend had explained that cloud-mining websites take in coinage, and about the time that amount of BTC the outfit took in is close to the amount paid out to miners, they usually close up shop and are gone. I am not saying *all* cloud mining websites are doing this, but beware. In theory they sound great, but in practice, they aren't so sustainable. Greed is what will destroy you in this world of finance. If someone actually had that kind of mining capacity, they would simply use it for themselves if it were as profitable as they say it is.

Everyone who is outside of the United States may avail themselves to many online options for buying Bitcoin such as www.coinbase.com. Maybe in the future these types of exchanges will support U.S. customers, but it just depends on whether they are willing to comply with the Patriot Act and anti-money laundering laws, or risk our government going after them. Maybe some of these places already do accept U.S. customers for buying BTC, but I have not yet seen it. Oh, it is possible for some exchanges, but U.S. customers are not allowed to register for all or some of the payment methods. There is no easy way around this red-tape I am afraid.

An unorthodox way to buy Bitcoin, that you must feel free to disregard, which as an American (it is virtually impossible due to our idiotic laws congress has passed, to actually buy

BTC directly like most other countries get to do) happens to be my favorite: There are online casinos which payout in Bitcoin. If you have a gambling budget, and if you do gamble already, you might as well deposit with fiat and when you win, take the BTC as payment for your withdrawal.

If you deposit, and then turn around and cash out, they will usually take a fee for this, but as long as you play a little bit and then cash out, there usually is no fee. Do yourself a favor though, if you use this method (I only recommend it if you have a gambling budget you spend anyways as there are no fees on the coinage you withdraw if you've turned your balance over a few times in their games) be sure to fill out all required verification and authorization forms ahead of time and send them to the casino support department as instructed on their website or in the cashier. They will not process withdrawals until you've provided them a scan of your ID, card used for deposit, and the forms themselves. Typical processing time in my experience for BTC withdrawals has been twelve to twenty-four hours or less.

There are cryptocurrency-only based casinos, but I find their games are generally suspicious with odd and streaky results. The results at these casinos do not seem at all typical of fair and random gaming. Always try to stick to traditional online casinos who are licensed and regulated; not many of the purely crypto casinos are regulated and licensed. Some even operate with pirated casino software, or at least have done so in the past! If you must test any casino, try small amounts first. The only advantage to these crypto-only casinos is that payouts are virtually instant. If you are going to try to gamble as a method of gaining BTC, at least look into "Video Poker Profits from the Ground Up", and yes, I have won quite a few BTC in the past playing Video Poker for cryptocurrency, it was the only way I had at the time to obtain it, so I had no choice but to succeed.

I don't want to encourage non-gamblers to gamble, however. The average person does seem to already gamble, at least in America, and I'd say this makes up a vast majority of our population. The sooner our government realizes this fact, the sooner they might legalize it and regulate it rather than see foreign companies making all of the gaming profits, all Government is supposed to do is serve the people, not turn things into crimes which are not crimes; yet this is the kind of world we live in.

If you do decide to try casinos as a method to turn fiat money into BTC, I recommend Bovada.lv, or inetbet.com. Again these are not paid endorsements. Bovada has always paid me off when I cash in with a reasonable time frame of 24 hours or so, and they have a great assortment of games. They are also licensed and regulated. Inetbet.com has lightning fast customer support. If you email them, within a few minutes you usually have a detailed reply that is not a canned response. At this point, they have earned my respect and loyalty for being so proactive in taking care of their customer's needs. They also have very affordable slot tournaments with guaranteed cash prizes which run regularly.

We can buy eBooks, we can buy computer games, guess what? It is all bits of data. Do you know what else is all just bits of data? Cryptocurrencies. So why can't we buy Bitcoin as easily as we can buy a computer game? It doesn't make sense to me either, but I hope the words I write will find their way into the hands of people who can help make changes we desperately need in order that the very liberty our founding fathers fought and sacrificed for might someday be restored. Financial and economic liberty were of chief importance, and need to be again. We need to reassert our liberties which government had no right to take away from us in the first place.

The easiest option for Americans to buy BTC, is the costliest. www.virwox.com lets you deposit with credit cards, Paypal, or many other methods; they even let you sell BTC instantly and withdraw it to Paypal instantly. The problem is they layered the conversion fees. They ding you for around 10-

15% in fees when you turn your fiat into Second Life Lindens (SLL), and then another 10-15% when you turn the SLL into BTC. When you sell, the same thing happens. The last time I sold a Bitcoin on Virwox, BTC was worth $750.00. By the time I received the final amount, I had $580.00 to show for it. If you were to buy a Bitcoin on Virwox right now, a $10,000 Bitcoin will cost you closer to $13,000 due to the layered fees. Yes, they are reliable and trustworthy, but they have a sort of monopoly on serving U.S. customers and they seem to know it.

The internet is always changing, laws are always changing; who knows if they will change in our favor or not but my advice is to search the web for Bitcoin purchasing options for U.S. residents and keep looking for the best options you can find. If I am ever wrong about there not being excellent options, then I welcome that for the sake of our liberty, I *want* to be wrong about this one point.

One of my predictions for the future is that as Bitcoin climbs into the tens and hundreds of thousands of dollars each, banks may start selling them at their counters; banks sometimes have gold and silver desks, so why not cryptocurrency desks? Maybe some already do, but I think one day we will be able to buy BTC as easily as you can walk in and buy a postage stamp or a certificate of deposit. You see, they can't afford not to get in on this madness, and they know it. They surely must.

I cannot stress that just about any price is a bargain for Bitcoin. When BTC was $1,000.00 I avoided buying any, because I didn't want to have to spend $1200.00 or more on Virwox to buy a Bitcoin! Then it goes to $3,000.00 and I didn't buy any because I didn't want to pay $3600.00 for a Bitcoin. Now, I still will not use Virwox, I can't bring myself to pay $9,600.00 for a $8,000.00 Bitcoin. If I look at the trend, well, it is better to pay $9,600.00 for a Bitcoin than wait for it to go up to $25,000.00.

Actually, if your option is to pay $12,000 for a Bitcoin with which to begin investing, then maybe mining is a better option for you. That would build a couple very nice and powerful altcoin mining rigs! *(For $12,000, I could build enough mining rigs to pull around $20,000-$40,000 a year profit depending on the coin and market conditions currently.)* Better yet if you can mix it up and buy some coinage to not miss out on the cheap altcoins at present, and the trading opportunities, then set up a mining rig for the more lucrative altcoins, you are set!

No matter what choice you make, there are always options; so let us move on to the more lucrative method which costs as little or as much as you want to invest!

*** **Update*** **

Just since I finished this chapter about two days ago, before I could finish and publish this book, COAL in fact did rally as I said it was capable of doing. The chart from today, 11/27/2017 is presented at the end of this section showing the tremendous returns afforded by properly interpreting market signals and all other changes. There are perfect storms that occur from time to time, such as COAL had: A new and superior PC based wallet; established on a major exchange; extremely stable but low price with lots of support on the buy side; along with a very high mining difficult and very much mining hash-rate committed to it.

With 500 H/s (Hash/second, not the kind you smoke either) my computer was only able to mine around one COAL per hour, at under ten cents a coin, you will not be getting rich. For the record, network mining power was 250KH/s and block size was just over 12 COAL per block. What we are looking to do with altcoins is gather up any amount we can of the best looking coins, so that in the future, this ten cent coin I spent an hour mining will hopefully be a future value of hundreds of dollars!

COAL went from a daily trade volume of just about .01 BTC every twenty-four hours, to almost 10 BTC (with the price now over $9,800 that is quite the achievement) in mere days.

Update as of 11/30/2017: BTC has hit just shy of $12,000 a coin and has retreated to around $10,000 again. It will resume climbing, with as much certainty as anyone can have about anything.

The sky really is the limit at this point, and the fact the COAL price isn't crashing: If the price equalizes relative to mining difficulty, yes, it is a bonanza just waiting to happen.

It is best to not revise a whole book every day that something changes that I haven't published it; it is better to show you where things came from, and where they went to, so that you can learn to spot the trends and identify the specific quirks of the opportunity. Yes, every day this book isn't published is costing people time and opportunity, but would you believe in the opportunity if I could not prove it actually worked with all of these examples, and showing you what kinds of large changes there were between writing originally, revising, and actually proof-editing before uploading this to be published?

ADAM G. KOCH

PART VI: MINING & MINING RIGS

You have up until this point journeyed through the fundamental components of the opportunity itself and just what you are missing out on by not being involved as well as the basics of how trading and coin exchanges work. While buying BTC may not be your best option for a number of reasons, BTC is not cheap and it is going to become more expensive in the near future. If you buy coinage, it is up to you to grow it through investing and trading in altcoins, which is phenomenal. Otherwise, just holding onto BTC, it will take years for it to take you where you could have arrived much sooner; without all the extra BTC you would have made also.

However, if you invest in mining rigs they will return your investment many times over and after a few months or so the average mining rig can pay itself off leaving you to mine pure profit. Do you want a one-time return or something that pays you forever? This part of the book is going to explain the various types of mining, the benefits and drawbacks, and how to carry them out. Where possible I will give examples, however, so many currencies are implemented differently that you usually do not have a one-size fits all approach. Once you know how to mine one coin, though, it makes it much easier to figure out how the others work. You will never be left without the knowledge you need for making a specific crypto work for you; whether your wallet isn't working right or whether you can't figure out how to initiate mining software, the internet will tell you, all you have to do is ask it. If I were to teach you how to mine every different coin, we are talking a whole bookshelf of books! That is how many coins exist, each with their own oddities and specific instructions. Many currencies exist only as a command-line console application. Very confusing especially if you are not familiar with Microsoft DOS. (Disk Operating System for those of you who did not know.)

I am also going to give you a parts list for building your own super-duper mining rig a lot cheaper than you are going to be able to buy one with comparable mining power! The hardest thing there is, is to find the recipe for building something great, and I am lucky enough a good friend shared their list of materials they use to build their massive mining operations with. If you don't want to mess with building, I will cover the selling points you need to look at when buying, just so you can make an informed decision either way.

When you are done mining certain coins, there are always others worth pointing your mining rigs to. If you don't want to jump in so deep so fast, or if you do not have money to invest, you probably have a computer or a laptop which is enough to begin mining with. It is possible to mine a decent quantity of various altcoins just using a single computer, though with limited mining power you are going to need to find coins which are trading but easy enough to mine.

Pool mining guarantees you will get something for your effort; very rarely, particularly with brand new coins, can you solo mine entire blocks for yourself with just a computer. Even after the coin gains in popularity and difficulty, a more appropriate sized mining rig will still fairly easily let you solo mine blocks of coins.

There are two types of mining that can be done with a computer: CPU (Central Processing Unit) and GPU (Graphics

Processing Unit) mining and you can run them both at the same time.

CAUTION: Make sure your desktop computer has adequate cooling or your graphics could fail over time; GPU mining on a laptop is not recommended unless you have a cooling pad under it with additional fans. If you have a gaming laptop with a turbo cool feature such as MSI offers on their machines, there are seldom any issues with overheating. Also, do not rely on Solid State Drives to hold your cryptocurrency wallets. Make sure they are backed up to a magnetic drive, or a flash drive. My laptop shut off without warning one day, and the SSD was undetectable. The drive had failed completely just like that and if I did not have backups on other drives, I would have been wiped out of my currencies. I have a good friend who's sitting on eighty Bitcoins lost to a failed hard drive, which so far no lab has succeeded at recovering the wallet.

Certain coins are most efficiently mined with CPU's, such as Scrypt based coins (LTC, COPPER, and similar). The algorithm is not efficient for GPUs to tackle; you will see a slight increase in mined coinage but at the cost of a tremendous rise in consumed electricity.

ASIC's, short for Application–Specific Integrated Circuits, have saturated the mining sectors for Bitcoin and even Litecoin. If you have a Bitcoin ASIC, it can only be used to mine Bitcoin, even if you find a coin that is similar to Bitcoin. If you have a Litecoin ASIC, it should actually mine different Scrypt based cryptocurrencies including Litecoin, unless otherwise specified. While ASIC's are their own mining rig, they often do not have their own display and require being patched into a computer or network to operate.

It is most lucrative to operate mining rigs which are versatile and not locked in to one or two currencies due to the substantial investment this technology represents, and the fact it allows us to mine the largest variety of the coins which exist, means as market conditions change we can adapt to these new conditions if we stick to GPU based mining.

Keeping your options open is valuable in this ever-changing world, and if you want to mine Bitcoin or Scrypt based currencies, you can always do that at some point, too.

-Mining Coins With Your PC

Once you decide which coin you want to mine (browsing the exchange listings or looking up the various coins on coinmarketcap.com and even browsing the forums are good ways to find a currency you will wish to mine) go to the official webpage for that coin, or the official forum announcement and you will find the links and directions for getting the mining software, and setting it up. Like in the last chapter, I am going to choose an example and walk you through it here.

For the sake of brevity, and uniformity; I will use COAL as the example since I am most familiar with it; it actually is as profitable to mine now as Monero. However, if you can successfully make your machine mine COAL, (these directions are essentially the same for any XMR and Cryptonote type currency with minor changes), you should have a basic foundation from which to understand the steps involved in whatever mining you intend to do.

-FIRST STEPS:

You will want to install the PC wallet, until such time as a web wallet exists for the coin you are mining, anyways. You cannot mine directly to exchange wallets because as in the case of Cryptopia, they do not support "generated" transactions from pools. Coins can become lost if you try.

For the purpose of our example, you can download the GUI Bitcoal wallet from:

https://github.com/bitcoal/bitcoalwallet/releases

Naturally the link and software are subject to change. You can always find the proper working links on the official websites for the currencies or in the forums if you have no luck finding the official sites. Wallets are open source, so that anyone may at any time visually inspect the code for their peace of mind, and even compile it themselves to ensure there is no malicious security risk embedded in the software. Do not be alarmed if you get virus warnings; clean cryptocurrency software almost always generates false alarms.

Once you have downloaded the wallet program, you simply run it as you would any other program. Put the .exe file where you can find it, and make a shortcut to it because you will need to run it every time you want to launch the wallet. If you want to keep the blockchain backed up, along with your wallet, by default these files are stored in c:\users*yourusername*\appdata\roaming*coinname*. Just copy and paste the folder where you want to back it up to. Always store your backups in a secure location.

The wallet will download the blockchain consisting of all the past transactions made with that currency, and it will take sometimes minutes or hours depending on your computer speed and internet bandwidth. I would abstain from sending coins to your wallet before it synchronizes, in case it does not fully sync making your coins inaccessible until you find a way to make it sync. The synced COAL wallet is pictured below:

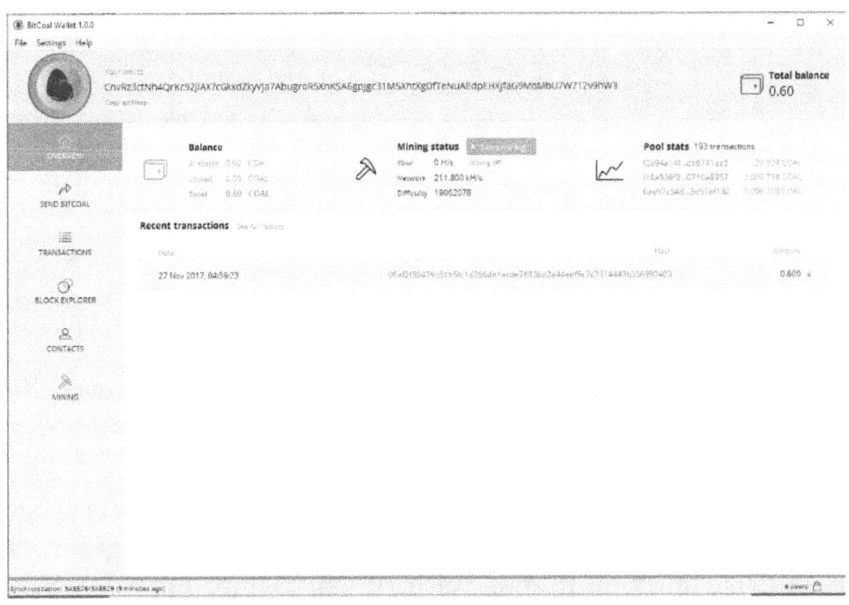

Notice the various features. You will need to utilize the wallet address provided for you in the upper left of your wallet when mining. Typically, your solo mining is done using the Command Line Interface wallet along with the provided software often called "minerd." For our purposes, we are looking at pool mining, and you will learn how to use a command line interface miner to do it.

Next, you are going to want to visit a mining pool, which is pictured below (point your browser to coal.mypool.online):

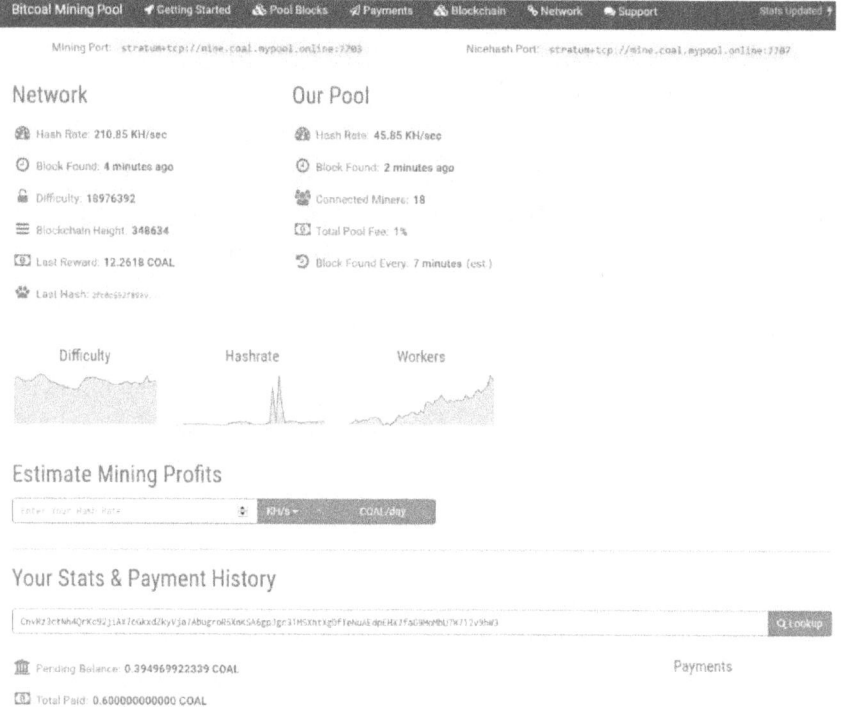

It is a straight-forward type of website. It shows the statistics for the pool and for the whole network, and also your mining history.

To put Hash Rate into perspective, my MSI GT62VR Dominator gaming laptop, has a nVidia 1060 6GB graphics card in it, fairly high end. With the xmrMiner provided as a suggestion to mine COAL with; I derive 450-500 Hashes per second. So, the chance of finding a block is really low with 18 million difficulty. I can run multiple graphics intensive games at full quality, such as *Entropia Universe* and *Fallout 4*, without bogging this laptop down or overheating it with the turbo cooler going. In fact, it runs nice and cool this way, which is important, heat can warp your motherboard and damage components and then you are out a computer! My Acer did it to two motherboards before I had to scrap it leaving me to buy this! I was playing games on low quality settings and still overheated the Acer; low end laptops do not cool efficiently.

If you look at the network mining rate, 210 KH/s, or Kilo Hashes, Kilo being a thousand of course. That is so much mining power, that I only have 475 on average, divided by 210,000 Hash per second... That is 0.22% of all mining power, so realistically, I will only find a fifth of a percent, or less, of all blocks mined if I were to solo it. Pool mining will yield less than 0.22% of the future coins mined as long as I am running. It is hard to justify using my laptop to mine such little coinage when I can mine speculative amounts of new currencies instead. The list of parts for the rig I was given is for a rig which lets you run up to thirteen GPU's. There are many more powerful GPU's than what I currently have in my laptop. When you have this kind of hash rate, you will be able to mine a significant value of whatever coin you point the miner to, especially, and I can't stress this enough, newly released currencies which are ripe for mining mountains of them for little cost and time.

The difficulty is dynamic, since blocks are randomly found, so the difficulty adjusts in order to maintain a specific block time, if blocks are very rare, difficulty drops so it becomes easier until it averages out. Cryptonote block rewards taper off slightly with each mined block instead of halving, making them slightly smaller until the final block is cracked, after which the network is left to earn only from transaction fees. This leads to a more stable rate of increase than halving.

As a rule of thumb a lot of miners, and a lot of mining power is a sign that the coin is very much alive and is not going to die any time soon. A large increase in mining will raise the prices of the coin. The stronger the mining power reaches, the higher the potential price. Hash rate drives market values to a large degree.

If you go to the "Getting Started" page (the link is found at the top of the site), you will find what is essentially an "easy start" guide. Several mining software's will be listed, with the directions on how to use the command line. If there are configuration files, or .bat files to edit for launching the mining software, there will be comments along with self-explanatory variables to change for everything to work properly for you. Pictured below is the list of mining software and their various directions to use them.

Mining Apps

App Name	Architecture	Downloads	Discussion	Source Code
XMR-Stak-CPU (by fireice_uk)	CPU	Github	Reddit	Github
Example: xmr-stak-cpu Please edit config.txt file to suit your needs.				
XMR-Stak-AMD (by fireice_uk)	OpenCL (AMD)	Github	Reddit	Github
Example: xmr-stak-amd Please edit config.txt file to suit your needs.				
CPUMiner (forked by LucasJones & Wolf)	CPU	Github	BitcoinTalk	Github
Example: minerd -a cryptonight -o stratum+tcp://mine.coal.mypool.online:7703 -u YOUR_WALLET_ADDRESS -p x				
YAM Miner (by yvg1900)	CPU	MEGA	Twitter	Proprietary
Example: yam -c x -M stratum+tcp://YOUR_WALLET_ADDRESS:x@mine.coal.mypool.online:7703/xmr				
Claymore CPU Miner	CPU	MEGA	BitcoinTalk	Proprietary
Example: NsCpuCNMiner64 -o stratum+tcp://mine.coal.mypool.online:7703 -u YOUR_WALLET_ADDRESS -p x				
Claymore GPU Miner	OpenCL (AMD)	MEGA	Discussion	Proprietary
Example: NsGpuCNMiner -o stratum+tcp://mine.coal.mypool.online:7703 -u YOUR_WALLET_ADDRESS -p x				
ccminer (forked by tsiv)	CUDA (Nvidia)	Github	BitcoinTalk	Github
Example: ccminer -o stratum+tcp://mine.coal.mypool.online:7703 -u YOUR_WALLET_ADDRESS -p x				
xmrMiner	CUDA (Nvidia)	Github	Forum	Github
Example: xmrMiner_0.2.0.exe --url=stratum+tcp://mine.coal.mypool.online:7703 -u YOUR_WALLET_ADDRESS -p x --bfactor=8 --bsleep=100				

xmrMiner worked very easily for me, and it should like I said, work on any Cryptonote based currency as long as you properly edit the files. Depending on your graphics card manufacturer, your availability of software is limited, since AMD and nVidia use different architecture and all. When source code is listed as "proprietary", they are usually mining software built with a compulsory donation scheme, whereby a portion of your mining is done for the creator of the software. Most mining software is free and open-source.

To download your mining software, as I have nVidia graphics, I had to click on the "github" link for xmrMiner, and it takes you to the download page. Once downloaded, extract it to a location you want to put it. I try to keep all mining and software running from a magnetic hard drive or a flash drive, to prevent premature failure of my SSD drive. Right click on xmrMiner_easystart.bat file, and click edit:

```
rem the word "rem" at the beginning of a line is a line with a comment
rem please substitude with you Monero adress
set
xmrAddress=CnvRz3ctNh4QrKc92jiAX7cGkxdZkyVja7AbugroR5XnKSA6gpJgc31MSXhtXgDfT
eNuAEdpEHXJfaG9MoMbU7W712v9hW3

rem passwort for your mining pool (very often only a x)
set poolPassword=x

rem mining pool webaddress
set poolUrl=url=stratum+tcp://mine.coal.mypool.online:7703

rem set here the launch param to tune xmrMiner (see xmrMiner_VERSION.exe --help), e.g. --launch=8x3
rem example: set launchParam=--launch=64x3
set launchParam=

rem greater value means more interactivity of your system but lower hash rate
set bFactor=6

rem time between a kernel start
set bSleep=25

xmrMiner_0.2.1.exe    --url=%poolUrl%    -u    %xmrAddress%    -p    %poolPassword%
%launchParam% --bfactor=%bFactor% --bsleep=%bSleep%
pause
```

I want to apologize to eBook customers, I cannot guarantee that example is going to come out looking the way it is formatted, but even if it is run together, you should be able to understand what is going on when you compare it to your file in front of you on your computer.

Usually the only changes you need to make, is to add your wallet address, and properly input the URL for the mining pool server as shown. Do not tamper with the last few lines with the percent marks. The last part of the file, the xmrMiner_0.2.1.exe may not be the same name as your exe, because of different versions and a .bat that was not updated as such; so just make sure that part of the file matches the name of the .exe file. There are settings you can tinker with to affect Hash Rate, but over time knowing how to adjust things is something that comes from research and learning from forums along with trial and error.

When you launch the .bat file, a console window will open, and it will automatically begin mining with your settings. As long as it runs, it will be generating and submitting shares to the mining pool with each share earning you some portion or another of a given coin.

Congratulations! Now you know how to mine your first cryptocurrency! The miner that is built into the wallet is only a CPU miner, you will not make much, but mining with your GPU effectively gives 10x more mining power, at least for me on this particular computer. It takes time for blocks to be found, and shares to be paid out so just be patient.

Sometimes you manually have to start mining, as there is no .bat file or configuration file to edit. In this instance, you can achieve the same results by copying the example command from the "getting started page" for your software of choice, and pasting it into notepad; from there you will copy and paste your wallet address into the command. Once done, open Command Prompt from your Start menu. If you make it a small window, and then open a small window with the folder containing your mining software, click and drag the xmrMiner_0.2.1.exe file onto the command prompt is the easiest way to launch. Otherwise, simplify the folder name to "xmrMiner", and move it to say D:\ (C:\ if you only have one hard drive). Then in the command prompt you would in this example type "CD D:\xmrMiner\xmrMiner_0.2.1.exe" to launch it. Once it is running, you need to copy and paste your command with your wallet address into the window, and hit enter. You should now be mining!

Whatever mining software you use, do not worry, there will be instructions somewhere telling everything you need to know, just take it one step at a time and you will get through it!

The pool also has a mining calculator; right now my 500 H/s is calculated to pull 28 Bitcoal a day when I entered my Hash rate. You may have to click the drill down menu to change from KH/s to H/s. Your mining software will tell you the Hash rate you are mining with.

Wallet addresses should always be copy and pasted, they are so complex and case-sensitive, meaning it is virtually impossible to manually type them, and it is so time consuming to do. You will save a lot of headache copy and pasting. Cryptonotes make use of a second code sometimes in addition to your wallet address, if offered by a wallet you are sending to, you need to insert this into the second field when sending.

-Mining Rigs

These can range from hundreds of dollars to tens of thousands of dollars. By and large, the most expensive part of these, are the graphics cards. So many graphics cards are sold for mining cryptocurrencies, that the gaming community who only want the cutting edge graphics for actually playing games cannot find any to buy. The newest and greatest cards sell out in the blink of an eye, because whoever has the most efficient most powerful hardware has a chance at taking a greater share of the mined coins than the other miners with older hardware.

eBay is a good source for buying mining rigs, but you may overpay if it is a "Buy it Now" listing; an auction is more honest, people will not bid more than they can buy the same thing elsewhere for, so you almost certainly will pay fair market value for whatever rig you do buy. Amazon is good too, and any website where they actually protect the buyer in case something goes wrong and you have recourse to ask for a refund or whatever measures are necessary to make it right.

The primary concerns in buying mining rigs are to get the most Hash Rate for the least power consumption for the lowest price per Hash. All of these are specifications you can write out on a piece of paper for each one you are looking at, and whichever one makes the most sense for you is the one you want. There are many choices for the various price ranges, and as technology changes, you can swap the older graphics cards out and buy newer cards while selling the older ones to defray the cost of the upgrade; so a mining rig can change with the times. ASIC's however, are generally not something you can just upgrade or otherwise alter.

If buying from any online seller, always review their feedback and pay special attention to the negative reviews and feedback left; some types of complaints exist which do not necessarily mean you should avoid doing business, but always look for the most reputable sellers to deal with and any issues that most impact your certainty of a good purchase.

Cryptonote coins are generally rated in H/s. Bitcoin miners are rated in MH/s and TH/s, that is Mega hash and Terra hash per second. Zecash uses Solutions per second. If you go to www.coinwarz.com, you will find a large assortment of cryptocurrency calculators. Not all currencies are available here, but it will give you an idea of what your rig is capable of earning you.

I did a search on eBay and randomly selected an example of a mining rig for you. For $3,399.00, there is a 6-GPU mining rig capable of 172MH/s (ETH mining rate, 1,750

Solutions/second for Zecash, 4,200 H/s for cryptonote) suitable for mining Ethereum and Zecash and Cryptonote currencies, for sale. The power consumption is listed as 900-1,150 Watts depending on what you mine. Where I live, electricity is around 9.5 cents per Kilowatt hour. My cost to operate this miner would run around $2.50 a day, which isn't so bad. Now, we can take this information and plug it into the coinwarz.com calculators.

As of 11/27/17, the profitability charts are as follows for these specs, and yes, they will change, and your actual results will vary. This is only provided as an educational aid to give you an idea of what you can expect from making such investments in hardware for mining purposes. You will need to crunch the numbers yourself when the time comes to buy a mining rig. As long as it will pay itself off in a fairly short period of time, it is a good investment.

Ethereum (ETH) (0.048 BTC per coin @ $9,995.00 BTC)
Hourly: 0.00123240 ETH produced w/ ~$0.50 USD Profit
Day: 0.02957766 ETH produced w/ ~$12.07 USD Profit
Week: 0.20704362 ETH produced w/ ~$84.51 USD Profit
Month: 0.88732978 ETH produced w/ ~$362.18 USD Profit
Year: 10.79584567 ETH produced w/ ~$4,406.48 USD Profit

Profit does not include the costs of the mining rig, only power consumption at $0.09 per Kw/hr. It would take just under a year for this particular mining rig in the above example with current market and mining conditions, to pay for itself. It could be greatly reduced, or lengthened depending on how strong or weak the coin becomes in relation to Bitcoin. But, in terms of comparing how profitable it is to mine this versus another coin, you will see how these calculators can improve your earnings by finding the most profitable coin. Also, you may obtain a great deal more mining power out of a rig if you use different software or configure it differently than the original owner had used it.

Monero (XMR)(0.01826059 BTC per coin @ $9,995.00 BTC)

Hourly: 0.00284594 XMR produced w/ ~$0. 43 USD Profit
Day: 0. 06830267 XMR produced w/ ~$ 10.30 USD Profit
Week: 0.47811870 XMR produced w/ ~$ 72.08 USD Profit
Month: 2.04908015 XMR produced w/ ~$ 308.93 USD Profit
Year: 24.93047519 XMR produced w/ ~$ 3,758.65 USD Profit

As you can see, this may not be the best rig, as there are other mining setups which offer a much shorter Return on Investment (ROI), which is only a measurement of how long until you actually have your first profits. Either that, or the person who owned and operated the rig had it misconfigured and were not utilizing the full capacity of the graphics cards in the most efficient way. The best metric perhaps of what the most profitable mining rig for you is, would be the ROI. The sooner a rig can pay itself off, the more efficient it is and the more money it will be making for you! However, let me use this to teach you another valuable point!

COAL is the same type of coin that Monero is. (No it's not the *same* coin obviously, but similar.) It reduces in block size over time, difficulty goes up with mining power, also. While 28 COAL does not sound like much right now at 0.00000700 of BTC per coin, but imagine how grateful you will be to mine a year's worth of coinage in a day? Once upon a time, it was possible to mine 28 XMR in a day, also, but those times are long passed. Someday COAL will be as difficult to mine, so, for speculating, even if you only get a few coins of something that is hard to mine, someday it will be much harder to obtain those same amounts of coins. Actually, COAL and XMR run nearly equal in terms of BTC value of coinage generated by the same rig, give or take a little, if this trend continues, we are in good shape, eventually.

In the choice between the two examples of coins I calculated for the example presented, you would want to mine Ethereum, then just keep your eye on the markets and change to which coin is most profitable. That is if you are only mining to show a profit. As I said before, a lot of our opportunity is not in those coins that are great, it is in those coins which will rise to greatness. What is the *next* Monero, or Ethereum, or any of the other valuable coins? I do think COAL is the next Monero, and I am working on putting my money where my mouth is. I don't want you to just take what I say at face value, do your own research and make the best use of the knowledge I have provided you as guidance.

Cryptocurrency is a natural opportunity as everyone can access the markets, everyone can participate. Sure, you can apply my principles to buying and selling old stamps, or gemstones, or any manner of things; but you have to find the market to be successful, you can't trade a spread on anything if there is no market for you to sell what you buy to. Cryptocurrency, and even stocks, live on the internet, meaning it is right at the end of our fingertips any time we have an internet capable device before us. There is no market to find, it is just there waiting for anyone who wants in on it.

The best advice I can give you, is try to mine a quantity of every fairly reliable altcoin you can, a quantity that *if* and *when* the value rises to what you predict it may, you will be happy with the proceeds from selling or using those speculated coins, and maybe never sell *all* of your coins, but by all means sell them in stages, because the sky literally is the limit with something so limited, and when something goes viral there is no putting a ceiling on it again. Just look at Bitcoin! So, diversify! Experiment! Research! Whatever you do, give yourself the best possible chance at being in the running for a life-changing success!

-Building a Mining Rig: Parts List and Basics

If you do not want to buy a mining rig, you may build one. This is recommended for people who are do-it-yourself friendly. It should be fairly straight forward, like building a desktop computer. That said, if you have never built a desktop computer, you will have to do some self-study on how to assemble these components properly and what software is needed to run the rig.

I am still collecting the parts to build mine, but as promised, here is the parts list to build a monster of a mining rig. The basic components are not very costly; it is the graphics cards that will be costly. It is very possible to just add them as you can afford them, a card a month or every two months. Occasionally rigs do appear that are cheaper to buy than to build, but they don't last long so if you are looking online, be prepared in case you see a deal you can't afford to let go of.

It is difficult to know what parts to buy, and have a working rig at the end of the whole process. Parts have to be compatible; processors have to have the right socket on the motherboard, etc. I haven't personally built this rig yet or I would go step by step on the assembly and making it operational. I apologize I can't go into greater depth here because of that. There are a lot of forums with a lot of help if you have specific questions about any phase of building your rig. For me, the hardest part was knowing what parts to buy in the first place, but setting them up should be simple enough.

I know everything which I know by jumping in and doing, and finding out how to do something; learning everything I could from anyone I knew I could ask. The hands-on approach is the best way to learn and understand what it is you are doing and why this part connects to that part and how it all works. I don't know if I would be doing you a favor by not giving you some homework. You can and probably should learn how rigs are assembled, and what is needed prior to buying your parts. It is out of the scope of this book in the first place, which it may seem like a small book, but it has taken far more time than all of my other books combined to finally finish! I am offering this parts list as a courtesy to my readers. The people who build mining rigs do not share their secrets if they can help it because many of them rely on being able to sell ready-made rigs for good markup, which yes, you could also if you had all the mining capacity you want already.

At the very least, you will have a starting point with which to calculate the cost to buy the parts to build a rig versus buying one already made.

PARTS LIST

PART	Qty.	Appx Price Ea.	Notes
ASROCK H110 PRO BTC+	1	$134	Motherboard
Intel Pentium G4400 CPU	1	$50	Processor
Heatsink/Fan for G4400	1	?	If it doesn't come with CPU, buy
Kingston Hyperx Fury 8gb	1	$50	RAM (Memory)
M.2 Solid State Drive	1	$75	128GB is plenty.
EVGA 750 GQ 750w	?	$90	1 per 4 to 5 GPU cards
AC769 PCI-E Riser	?	$10	1 per GPU card
Add2psu	2	$16	Connects extra power supplies
Frame	1	$100	For mounting parts to as solid unit
Graphics Cards	13	$200+?	Depends how high end of GPU

It is not so complicated, should be as easy as building a desktop computer but with slight differences. Instead of a solid enclosure, you will need to shop for a mining rig frame, and while this particular configuration is said to support up to thirteen graphics cards, I do not find frames supporting more than a dozen cards, although they may exist, so you will have to work out how you want to set that up. Two smaller frames next to each other, or maybe you can find a large frame. Frames can even be built if you have tools and materials, and there may be blueprints out there. I was told you could support thirteen GPU's with this rig design, but like I said, I have yet to build it.

The motherboard is what everything interfaces with. The CPU specified in the list is well matched for this board. You will need to buy a cooling fan / heatsink for the processor if you buy a processor that is not in a combo package already containing one. Sometimes they are sold together, other times they are separate, and you cannot run without one. Also make sure you have a tube of heatsink compound; some are better than others, and it is all fairly cheap so get the best you can if it isn't ridiculously overpriced.

Then you have the 8GB RAM, it is the temporary memory the computer uses so that it can quickly access and change data it is in the process of using; a hard-drive only computer would be very impractical. Hash Rate can go up slightly if you have two sticks of the same exact brand and model, I am told.

The M.2 Solid State Hard Drive does not have to be very large, but 128GB is a good size. You will want to back-up everything regularly, primarily your wallets need to be put in a safe place in case the SSD dies. Actually keeping copies of the wallet files themselves on a flash drive in a safe location is fine; if it is the same file, it doesn't matter when it was backed up your coins will still be there.

One power supply known as a PSU is needed per four or five graphics cards depending on how powerful the cards are. Since you can only attach one such power supply to a motherboard, you will need the Add2psu adapters, two of them.

The frame is what everything attaches to, and are usually open-air to facilitate cooling and preventing the buildup of heat which is very damaging to electronics. The cooler the mining rig is running, the better.

Unfortunately new graphics cards are coming out all of the time. You will want to do some searching on the web to find out what you can about the results people are having with different cards and brands of cards. There are many tables out there with side by side comparisons of Hash Rates for a large variety of GPU's and brands.

You should now have a basic understanding of mining sufficient enough to get you started with figuring out how you want to proceed with the opportunity at hand.

PART VII: CLOSING THOUGHTS

The very opportunity itself is the primary focus of this book which is why it was given the most depth and coverage, but I even expanded the scope of this literature to include actual instructions for the mechanisms which are central to the opportunity since I felt it was necessary to do so in order facilitate your journey through this world of cryptocurrency. This is intended as a basic guide and should have given some understanding to the phenomenon as a whole and the significance thereof. You will no doubt still have questions; but at least you now know what those questions and concerns are so that you may be able to put them into words and continue your learning experience by trying to answer them.

Start out small if you feel it best. As your confidence builds from experiencing some success, you will feel better about scaling up and going big-time. The more confident you are, the greater your successes may be. It can be overwhelming for the first week or two, but soon mining and trading cryptocurrency will become as natural as breathing air.

Cryptocurrency is such a broad subject, if I were to go into extreme depth, we literally are talking a whole library of books and the only thing larger than this phenomenon is its future importance. Cryptocurrency hit the world stage about seven and a half years ago, with Bitcoin running from a fraction of a cent to over $11,000.00 a coin: It was something we lived fine without having in the world eight years ago, but now it is so important that it is approaching the value of ten ounces of gold per coin quickly! This is astounding! A single Bitcoin now has the same purchasing power that $200 in gold had before and up until 1933! People were often earning only a nickel a day in the late twenties and early thirties because times were so tough, and that was only if they could find work! Think about that for a moment!

Do not be deceived by fake-news outlets trying to downplay this booming market. It will not take generations for Bitcoin to go to $50,000.00 or even $100,000.00, only a paltry few years could do it; and a million-dollar Bitcoin is very much possible in the same few years. Just imagine that after seven and a half years, many new businesses are still struggling to run a profit! There is no company in the world which could start off by issuing millions of penny shares, and in this same amount of time have the share price rise to $10,000-$12000, so yes it is a stellar success. We can only know the future by what the history shows us; there is no better time than now to do something to become part of this financial revolution.

There are countless books out there on the subject, but I do not write like other author's do. I have an entirely different style and approach when writing non-fiction and I very much hope that I have brought to you a unique point of view, with different insight and knowledge than any other author who writes on this subject ever could. I haven't read any of their books on the topic, so I assure you all of this came from my own working knowledge and experience as well as my one-on-one interactions with other people who were kind enough to share everything that they knew with me when I was as new to all of this as you might very well be now.

I have had to read so many boring books over the years, that I absolutely refuse to write one which is dry, uninteresting, or boring. My metric for whether or not I publish a book is simple. For one; does it meet my objective adequately? Yes, I would say this does. For another; am I proud to put my name to it and say this is the best that could be done? I really do think so. I will not publish unless it is the kind of book I feel that I would be happy buying and reading myself and afterwards feel like I received a great value for the investment. You really can't miss; I've handed you everything you need to know to turn rags into riches, and it cost you what, a cup or two of espresso?

This is the whole Jack and the Beanstalk all over again! Some people will think you bought a handful of worthless beans until you plant them and climb up there and start tossing those big shiny Bitcoins down from the clouds. I profited a whole BTC in the past week while editing this manuscript, from selling altcoins I had bought cheaply, even with the BTC hitting the all-time-high. I did not use any mechanism or strategy that is not found within this book. I rebought the amount of altcoin I sold when it crashed, and still have 750BTM's left over to put wherever I need to. This isn't a system; this isn't a gimmick; this book is the real deal.

There are already scores of people lining up to buy this book a month before it is even ready to be published! Many of them I know, many others whom I don't know; I owe it to them, and to you also, to have done the best possible work that I can do in giving you the principles upon which my current and future success is built. This is how the world is changed for the better; teaching people *how* to view opportunity, and to even find it at all so that they can replicate the steps involved in making success happen.

Do not let anyone sway your decision to look into this opportunity; in my experience the average person would rather see you suffer through life because they are so bitter that they themselves spent their lives being angry and narrow minded all while barely scraping by. No one wants to be in last place, the average person likes thinking they are in a better position than the other person. There are people who will take their anger from their own lack of achievement, out on you for actually making it somewhere in life. The common theme throughout society is, "if I can't succeed, I don't want you being successful either," and it is so wrong. Hopes and dreams are smashed in their infancy by people with these attitudes and so often the victims lose their motivation and ambition. There is nothing worse to take away from any human being (except liberty) than their ambition. How many of you are working a certain career or job only because your parents demanded you take it up? I am certain it is not a small number of my readers.

This book was written for all of you; you are holding in your hands the keys that will unlock your freedom to do what you wish in life, not what you were pressured to; it should at least ease your hardships and burdens if you will seriously consider what I have written and make use of the wisdom and knowledge provided in the best manner you can. This whole book is about improving liberty and quality of life for all who will listen and commit to doing something more than that which they typically are doing. I have put over a thousand hours into this project: The outlining, and thinking process; the half a dozen rough drafts; several entire rewrites; and the proof editing alone literally took a week of sixteen-hour days to complete. I have done everything I can, now it is your turn. It is up to you to make the difference in your own life just as I was able to make the difference in mine.

No it isn't a perfect book, I know that. I do think it is a good book or I would not be publishing it. I would argue that writing style, along with all of its punctuation and grammar usages whether right or wrong, in many ways are to a book what a finger is to a fingerprint; individuality is not a bad thing. I would bet money that if you gave two English experts the same manuscript, they would not make the same changes over the course of an entire book nor would they themselves be a hundred-percent accurate in regard to all the rules of the

English language. I have tried to present an every-day guide to every-day people as best I could, in a manner which everyone should be able to read, understand, and benefit from.

If you knew how disorganized I am as an individual and how many trains of thought I have running at the same time, once in a while on the same track heading towards each other, you would be amazed at what I have actually accomplished in completing this. It is so easy to look at a relatively small book and esteem it lightly; but I cannot quantify to you how much labor actually goes into even a "small book" such as this.

It is now time for me to sign off and leave you to figuring out how you shall proceed in building your cryptocurrency empire. I wish you all the best of luck, success, and prosperity in whatever you decide to do. I also now leave you with a couple of old quotations to ponder:

"Money is the life and soul of mortal men. He who has not heaped up riches for himself wanders like a dead man amongst the living." –Timocles

"Money glistens, adorned with virtue, it supplies the means by which thou mayest act well in whatever circumstances fate may have in store for thee." –Pindar

ABOUT THE AUTHOR

Born in the Pacific Northwest in 1985, having lived his whole life there; in addition to writing books the Author pursues various interests too numerous to list which no doubt will become the topic of future books. The Author's primary interests are gold prospecting, metal detecting, and online gaming along with countless other activities. The Author favors spontaneity over routine, aiming to make every day a different one.

The Author can be followed on Twitter: @goldbaron357

Author's other published books consist of:
Gold Prospecting & Placer Deposits: Finding Gold Made Simpler
Video Poker Profits from the Ground Up
Coin & Bullion Scams Exposed
Philatelic Philosophy: Stamp Collecting Wisdom & Opportunity
Technology Shopper's Guide: Saving You from Caveat Emptor

Some of the Author's current favorite cryptocurrencies:
Bitcoal (COAL) www.getbitcoal.org
Coppercoin (COPPER) www.coppercoin.com
BitcoinFast (BCF)
Gold Pressed Latinum (GPL)
Ethereum (ETH)

www.ingramcontent.com/pod-product-compliance
Lightning Source LLC
Chambersburg PA
CBHW051701170526
45167CB00002B/494